BARRON'S PAREN

KEYS TO BECOMING A FATHER

William Sears, M.D.

Pediatrician,
Assistant Clinical Professor of
Pediatrics at the
University of Southern California

BARRON'S

New York • London • Toronto • Sydney

Cover photo by COMSTOCK INC.

All inquiries should be addressed to:
Barron's Educational Series, Inc.
250 Wireless Boulevard
Hauppauge, New York 11788

Library of Congress Catalog Card No. 90-23988

International Standard Book No. 0-8120-4541-6

Library of Congress Cataloging in Publication Data

Sears, William, M.D.
  Keys to becoming a father / by William Sears.
    p. cm.
  ISBN 0-8120-4541-6
  1. Fatherhood—United States. 2. Fathers—United States.
3. Parent and child—United States. I. Title.
HQ756.S43 1991
306.874'2—dc20   90-23988
                                                        CIP

PRINTED IN THE UNITED STATES OF AMERICA
1234 5500 987654321

93263√

CONTENTS

INTRODUCTION

O ver the past decade, a father's role in child care has changed—for the better. As more and more women either choose to or are required to share in the family income, fathers must by necessity share in child care—a role many fathers wish, but are not comfortable doing. The main theme of this book emphasizes that a father's relationship and input with his child is not better than a mother's, not less than a mother's; it is *different* from a mother's. It is this difference that benefits the baby.

For centuries, fathers have been portrayed as well meaning but bumbling in their efforts to care for babies. Fathers are not just substitute mothers. They have their own unique input in the growth and development of their child.

Another myth is that only mothers are sensitive nurturers. How wrong! In this book I point out the importance of fathers becoming sensitive nurturers, and practical ways to achieve this quality. Throughout these Keys, I share with dads uniquely male nurturing tips that I have learned in fathering our seven children, and some time-tested baby comforting tips that other fathers have shared with me. I also will pass on knowledge gleaned from my 20 years in pediatric practice and from my consulting work with parents.

In the you-can-have-it-all commercial world, fathers are torn between professional success and family success. Dads,

1

let me share a realistic fact of fathering life with you, which, pitifully, took me six children to discover—you can't have it all. Women can't; neither can men. Some juggling between work and home is necessary. Fathers feel the economic pressure to put bread on the table, yet often do not have enough time to be present at the table. I present to you some practical career juggling tips to help you handle this dilemma.

An important point that I mention throughout many of the Keys is the concept of mutual giving—as you give to your baby, your baby gives back to you. Nothing matures a man like becoming an involved, caring father.

1

~~~~~~

FATHERING THE PRE-BORN BABY

athering begins before birth. A father may feel that after conception, it's the mother's job to carry the baby throughout pregnancy and there is nothing for him to do until baby is born. Wrong! As the mother cares for your pre-born baby, you care for the mother. Anything you can do to help your wife have a healthier pregnancy indirectly contributes to the health of your baby. The following are some specific tips on how fathers can contribute to the health of their baby—and their marriage—even before the baby is born.

Bond with your baby before birth. It is much easier for a mother to bond with her baby because the baby is a growing part of herself. With each month, she senses more and more her baby's presence within herself. It is very easy for the father to feel left out because nothing is happening to his body (although some men do relate that they experience pregnancy-like symptoms during their wife's pregnancy). Here are some ways to really get hooked on your baby before birth. *Talk to your baby prenatally.*

A recent area of fascinating research, called fetal awareness, has shown that the pre-born baby actually can hear sounds outside the womb by the sixth month of pregnancy, and perhaps earlier. Some researchers suspect that the pre-born baby actually may hear the father's voice better than the mother's, because the amniotic fluid transmits the resonant low-pitched male voice more easily than a higher feminine voice. Talking to your pre-born baby breaks the ice and makes it easier to talk to your baby immediately after birth. Studies have shown that babies whose fathers talked to them before birth attended more to their father's voices soon after birth, perhaps indicating that the sound of the father's voice had been imprinted on the mind of the pre-born baby.

The laying on of hands. This is a custom we have enjoyed during our last four pregnancies. (I use the term "ours" because once I became more involved with my wife's pregnancy, I naturally began referring to the pregnancy as "ours.") Every night before going to bed I would lay my hands on "the bulge," as I affectionately began referring to the outward signs of our pre-born baby. (Ask your doctor to show you how to locate your baby's head, which usually is palpable by the sixth month of pregnancy.) Each night I would talk to my baby, such as "Hi baby, this is your daddy out here; I'm looking forward to seeing you; I love you." Simply let yourself go and your thoughts flow.

At first you may feel somewhat foolish, a grown man talking to a bulge. But after this initial awkwardness, you will become more comfortable with this nightly ritual. No one is going to hear you, except the people who count, and they will understand. Placing your hands on your wife's abdomen and talking to your pre-born baby accomplishes two important prenatal messages: *You are committed to your wife and you are committed to your baby.* The combination of a warm hand on Mommy and warm words for Baby affirms your commitments to these two special persons who will depend on you after the birth. When my wife, Martha, and I used to teach childbirth classes, I would encourage the expectant fathers to lay hands on and talk to their pre-born baby. Their wives would later tell me that every time their husbands embraced their baby, they felt that their husbands were embracing them too. They were overjoyed at the feeling of their husbands' commitment to the baby and to them. Studies have shown that one of the greatest ways a father can contribute to the emotional well-being of the pregnant mother is to give her the feeling that he is *truly committed to becoming a good father.*

Prenatal bonding is good for Dad, too. Fathers who have practiced talking to and laying hands on their pre-born babies relate that they feel closer to their babies both before and after birth.

Let me share with you my own feelings after a few months of trying these prenatal bonding rituals. During the last three months of our fourth pregnancy, I enjoyed the nightly ritual of bonding with our pre-born baby. After the birth of Erin, I couldn't get to sleep at night until I first went over and placed my hand on her head and talked to her. I was hooked on this ritual before birth and it became part of me after she was born. My commitment to fatherhood was easier after Erin was born because it began before birth.

2

~~~~~~

THE "PREGNANT" FATHER

Here are some practical suggestions on how you can help the mother-baby hormonal communication network and create a more peaceful womb environment for both. One of the new and exciting areas of research into fetal well-being is how the emotional state of the mother affects the emotional state of the growing baby. If the mother is relaxed, the baby is relaxed. It is felt that continued upset during pregnancy causes the mother to have a higher level of stress hormones, and these hormones may cross the placenta and enter into the baby. Fathers, keep in mind, *upset mothers can lead to upset babies.* A mother who enjoys a pregnancy relatively free of unresolved stress carries a baby who is also spared these stresses. Helping the pregnant mother to minimize the stress of pregnancy is where a sensitive husband can really shine. Here is how!

One of the best starts you can give your baby is to bring him into a home built on a *stable and fulfilled marriage.* One of the best ways you can help your wife relax and have a less stressful pregnancy is to give her the feeling that you truly are committed to her as a husband and to your baby as a father. Women have confided in me that the feeling of this dual commitment is one of the most satisfying feelings during pregnancy. Besides bonding with your pre-born baby during pregnancy, a bit of prenatal "bonding" is advisable with your wife. Pregnancy is not only a state out of which babies grow, it is also a time in a couples' marriage when the relationship should grow.

Take Inventory. Pregnancy is a good time to take inventory of your marriage relationship. *What needs to be improved?* If there are weak points in your marriage that need to be strengthened, expecting the arrival of a baby to heal old wounds is naive and unrealistic. Marriage problems that occur prior to and during a pregnancy are more likely to be intensified after the birth of the baby. You may feel, "Of course I love my wife during her pregnancy; this is a high point of our marriage!" The real issue is, *does your wife feel your commitment?*

Each day give your wife signs that you truly care for her: a rose, a kiss, a hug, doing something especially nice for her, taking over the household chores, driving her someplace to do something especially for her, anything you can do to give her the message, "I want you to be more comfortable during our pregnancy."

Be sensitive. One of the main complaints I hear from expectant mothers is, "My husband is not sensitive to my needs." At no other time in a woman's life are her emotions more labile, her needs more intense. Her needs for your sensitivity during this time are greatest. The pregnant mother does tend to make mountains out of molehills. Minor upsets that previously did not seem to bother her now become very upsetting.

Respect the nesting instinct. During the final month or two of your wife's pregnancy, expect her to devote much of her time and energy to stabilizing her nest. This is the time that pregnant women are especially sensitive to changes in the stability of their home—soon to be their nest. If at all possible, avoid major changes at this time. This is not a time

7

to change jobs, move into a larger house, or make any major change that will upset the nest. If a major change is necessary, such as a move, try to do this early in the pregnancy rather than soon before or after the baby is born. Remember, to upset the nest is to upset the mother and, possibly, the pre-born baby.

Show interest and involvement in the pregnancy. Attend as many of your wife's doctor visits as you can. Participate in the major decisions: choice of doctor, choice of birthing environment, choice of childbirth classes. Above all, attend childbirth classes together. Some fathers may consider these classes for mothers only, but they are equally important for father. You learn about the physical and the emotional changes that take place in your wife during pregnancy and you learn how you can be more sensitive to these changes.

Understanding the care and feeding of the pregnant mother, stabilizing your marriage, becoming more sensitive to your wife, and becoming more involved in the pregnancy all lead to giving your wife one of the most important messages during the family pregnancy—that you are *committed to fatherhood.* Developing and demonstrating this commitment is the most important role of the pregnant father.

3

NORMAL FATHER FEELINGS DURING PREGNANCY

There are a variety of normal feelings that most fathers experience during pregnancy. I have experienced some of the following feelings during our pregnancies, as have most dads. Learning to recognize these feelings as normal and coping with them is part of maturing as an expectant father.

Excitement. Perhaps the earliest feeling you may experience is that of being excited about the birth of your baby. The announcement of "honey we're pregnant!" should be the high point of your marriage. It is important for your wife to see you catch the spirit of her excitement.

Ambivalence. After the initial feeling of excitement, it is normal to begin to have some ambivalent feelings about how this new member of the family will affect your lifestyle, your marriage, your economic situation. How will you provide for your baby? Will you need to live temporarily on one income? Will you have enough time to be an "involved father"? *It is normal for fathers to begin imagining how the baby will affect their marriage.* Will there still be "dinners for two" or getaway trips? Many fathers will worry unnecessarily about long-term economic pressures, wondering how they will afford to send their child to college. It is normal at this time for them to question their adequacy as a father and a provider. I suggest that expectant fathers not dwell on fears about the future and how a baby may change their lifestyle and marriage. This unnecessary worry about the future may cause an otherwise jubilant father to focus more on what he is going to lose and how much he is going to have to sacrifice after the baby is born rather than the joy that the baby is going to bring into the family.

Dependency. The term "dependent" begins to take on real meaning with the first pregnancy. Most husbands do not really consider their wife as a dependent until the baby comes. Along with the feelings of how the baby will depend upon you comes the increasing realization that your wife is showing increasing dependence upon you during her pregnancy. These double responsibilities may make you question your ability to both care and provide for the baby and mother.

Pregnancy-like symptoms. Some expectant fathers actually experience pregnancy-like symptoms of weight gain, nausea, and mood swings. I remember experiencing a "fullness" during some of our pregnancies. I felt a sense of "completeness" as if my life had taken on more meaning. These feelings are most common as you dream about your baby (as expectant mothers often do) wondering what he/she will be like, how the baby will act, whether he will look like you.

Feelings of being left out. Some fathers complain that their wife is so preoccupied with the pregnancy that there is no time or energy left for them. It may help you to cope with these feelings if you understand the many changes that go on in your wife during her pregnancy.

Sexuality during pregnancy. The most difficult change for new fathers to adjust to is the difference in their wife's sexual responsiveness. The same hormones that are responsible for the development and nourishment of your baby now and after birth are the very hormones that cause tremendous fluctuations in a pregnant woman's sexual desires. During the first trimester of pregnancy, most women are less sexually interested and responsive because of fatigue and gastrointestinal upset. During the middle trimester, because mothers often feel better and have grown accustomed to being pregnant, a woman's sexual desires may actually increase. As a woman grows to feel better about herself, she may also feel better about sex. Midway through pregnancy it is common for an expectant mother to have a more heightened awareness of her own sexuality.

In the last trimester of pregnancy, most women's sexual desires diminish for several reasons: The tremendous changes in their bodies make them feel more awkward as a sexual partner; there may be an underlying fear of inducing premature labor (which could be discussed with her doctor), and fatigue sets in. Also, in the final months the nesting instinct begins causing a woman to concentrate on preparing her nest and thinking about her pre-born baby, not about sex. Your wife may be uninterested in sex in the final months of pregnancy because her hormones are directed to her pre-born baby. She may also forget that your hormones have not changed at all throughout pregnancy. As you become more aware of your own unsatisfied sexual needs, your wife may become painfully aware of her inability to satisfy them. *Here is where it is necessary to be mutually sensitive to each other's needs and show inventiveness in sexual techniques.*

4

A FATHER'S PARTICIPATION IN THE BIRTH

A father's participation in the birth of his baby finally has achieved long overdue status. I have experienced tremendous changes in a father's participation at birth over the last 24 years. When our first two babies were born, I waited patiently in the waiting room while everyone else played a role in helping to deliver the very persons I helped to conceive. With our next three babies I was present in the delivery room and involved in helping my wife through labor. With our sixth and seventh child I was really involved. Our birth attendant did not arrive in time for the delivery, so I was able to catch our sixth baby. I was the first person to lay hands on our son, Matthew. I dare not say, "I delivered Matthew" because my wife, Martha, is quick to correct me by saying, "I delivered, you caught." With our seventh child, under the guidance of the birth attendant, I was also able to catch our baby. No longer are fathers banished to the waiting room during one of the most important events of their lives. Here is how you can—and should—be involved in your wife's labor and the birth of your baby.

Should father be a labor coach? Here is where I take exception to childbirth classes that teach fathers to be "labor coaches." Men coach sports, not laboring women. I feel it is important for you to attend childbirth classes mainly to help you understand what is going on with the physical and emotional changes that occur in your wife during pregnancy and to help her progress in labor. But, with rare exception, have I not seen a father completely forget all the breathing exercises he learned during a childbirth class. Fathers can go to pieces during labor worrying that they may not remember what they learned in class and feeling that they have failed as a labor coach. Let me suggest a possible alternative: Hire a labor coach, called a *doula*. This doula, or labor support person, stays with your wife during the entire labor helping her change positions, and easing the discomfort of labor and speeding the progress. This doula is a woman, usually a mother herself, with midwifery training or especially trained and experienced in helping the laboring mother progress. This is a woman-to-woman experience. Meanwhile you, as a father, do what you do best—love your wife.

Do whatever you can to make your wife more comfortable. Rub her back, embrace her during contractions, if she wants to be embraced. Support her with pillows where she needs them. All during labor give your wife the message that you care about her comfort and you will do everything possible to help her. Being a labor coach is a role that some men are comfortable with; *loving their wife through labor is a role that all dads welcome.*

Play your part with the choice of where your baby will be born. One possibility is an LDR (Labor, Delivery, Recovery)—a room in a hospital in which you and your wife check in much like you would into a hotel. The couple labor in the room, deliver the baby in this room, and rest following delivery in this room. This is an alternative to some delivery setups in which the laboring mother is treated like a surgical patient laboring in one room, wheeled to a delivery room, and then moves on from the "operation" to a recovery room.

Another way you can help your wife is to take over all the logistics that are necessary to have a baby in today's hospitals. Your laboring wife should not be worried with handling paperwork and hassling with the attending personnel. A proper birth is much like a well-orchestrated symphony; there is a natural flow to it. Mother takes center stage, but Dad is the stage manager working with all the medical personnel to be sure they contribute to helping a mother's labor progress, not interfere with it. *It is important for the father to run interference against negative comments,* such as, "You only dilated one centimeter..." A laboring mother is very vulnerable to any suggestion that her labor may not be progressing correctly and that she is "failing."

Help create a peaceful nest. Sometimes labor rooms are too busy—too many well meaning friends and relatives coming in and out, distracting your wife from tuning in to her body. Sometimes it is necessary to stand guard against these intrusions (this prepares you for your guard role against too many energy draining visitors after the birth).

Help your wife's labor progress. Dads, appreciate that a laboring woman is equipped with all the signals within her body that tell her how to work with her body to help her labor progress. You can help her identify these signals and create the environment that enables her to tune into her body's signals and act accordingly. One of the ways you can do this is by encouraging your wife to move about the labor room during delivery.

You may assist the laboring mother by encouraging your wife to walk around comfortably during labor, stopping periodically during her contraction. She may embrace you as a support person. I have particularly enjoyed these labor embraces during the birth of our last few children, as I felt my

14

wife was really leaning on me during a contraction. No one else can perform this role as well as you. The number one mistake that most first time laboring mothers make is to spend too much time in bed on their backs. Being upright and moving may allow gravity to help bring baby down. Your role is to help your wife move comfortably.

The following is a letter from one of the fathers in my practice, describing his role at birth.

"When my wife went into labor I wanted to share her experience. I didn't want to feel the pain, of course; I was too chicken for that, but I wanted to experience (as much as I could as a male) the joy of giving birth. We had attended childbirth classes and learned a lot of technical maneuvers, but when the time came for me to 'perform' I had forgotten most of what I had learned and decided to act on my feelings and simply love her through this labor. Whenever my wife showed that a contraction was coming on, I would embrace her as gently as I could. She held her arms around my neck while I held one arm around her and placed my other hand on 'the bulge' as I had affectionately termed this little person inside. As she labored, I felt her arms squeeze me tightly and sometimes her fingers dug into my back. The more she dug in, the harder I could feel her uterine muscles contract. Her panting and breathing patterns, her clinging embrace, and the ever changing position of her uterus let my body sense, though indirectly, what her body was going through. She felt better having me there and I certainly wanted to be there. I really felt that I was playing a part in helping her labor progress. I got to 'feel' her labor, too, and it didn't hurt me a bit. What a trip!"

5

HOW FATHERS CAN BOND WITH THEIR BABY

O ver the last 10 or 20 years, the concept of bonding with the newborn baby has received a lot of attention. Most of this bonding has been focused on mother-infant bonding, with the father given honorable mention. Although mother-infant bonding certainly is important at birth, father-infant bonding is also important—*for the baby and for the father*. Bonding means the close attachment that a parent and newborn infant develop shortly after birth. Researchers who study parent-infant bonding have seen that parents who bond with their newborn immediately or soon after birth become closer to their baby in the following months. Meanwhile, long-term effects of parent-infant bonding are still open to question. *Bonding with your baby is a lifelong process*, a series of steps that are taken during the early days, months, and years to develop a close relationship with your infant and child. Bonding in the newborn period may give this relationship a head start.

Engrossment. Researchers who study the effects of father bonding have used the term *engrossment* to describe how the presence of a newborn baby can make the father totally preoccupied and absorbed in the care of that baby. Engrossment doesn't mean so much what the father does for the baby as what the baby does for the father. A father who is engrossed in his baby is totally absorbed in the baby's unique features. The father feels that his baby is distinctly different from other babies and can't wait to hold him, talk to him, and interact with him. Engrossment ties into a favorite theory of mine: A baby can bring out the best (and the worst) in parents. Engrossment takes involvement one step further; it is involvement to a higher degree. Martin Greenberg, in his book *The Birth of a Father*, discusses one of the meanings of the root word engross, which is to "make large." He relates that not only does a new baby become a large part of the father's life, but fathers themselves feel that they may have suddenly grown—they feel bigger, older, and stronger.

The father feels an increase in his sense of self-esteem and a stronger identity as a parent. As director of a newborn nursery, I have had the privilege of attending many deliveries. I have noticed that a father during and after delivery is completely captivated by this new life that he and his wife hold in their arms. Whereas the mother is focusing totally on her baby, the father views the mother-infant pair through a sort of wide angle lens, perceiving the oneness that still exists between mother and baby, even though birth has changed the manner in which this oneness is expressed.

Fathers are good nurturers. Fathers are often portrayed as well-meaning but bumbling. In the newborn period, mothers have been thought to be the only nurturers, whereas the father's main role is to nurture the mother as she nurtures the baby. However, studies have shown that fathers make good nurturers too! Fathers who are given the opportunity and are encouraged to take an active part in bonding with and comforting their newborns become just as nurturing as mothers. When fathers who have bonded with their newborns are studied, it is noticed that fathers touch, look at, talk to, and kiss their newborns just as often as mothers do. I have noticed that a father's nurturant responses may be a little less automatic and a little slower to unfold than a mother's; but fathers are capable of a strong bonding attachment to their infants during the newborn period. The reason that fathers have not been portrayed as sensitive nurturers is because they often have not been given the opportunity to care for their newborn in the early days after birth.

Bonding tips for fathers. Even before the birth of your baby, let the medical personnel, preferably your obstetrician and the nurse in charge, know that, unless prevented by medical complication, you wish to have private time with your baby immediately after birth. Suggest that the routine injection of vitamin K and the routine eye ointment be delayed until an hour after birth so that you can enjoy this prime time of bonding with your newborn. This special time should not be taken over by trivial hospital routines or medications that can wait. Immediately after your baby is born (after the dust has settled, as one father put it) your baby should be put, skin to skin, on your wife's breasts, and the three of you can embrace each other—the birth of a family. During this initial bonding time most babies are in a unique state of *quiet alertness*. Their eyes are wide open and receptive to their environment. They get to know *immediately* to whom they belong. Some 10 to 20 minutes later, it is usual for babies to fall into a deep sleep. This state of quiet alertness is a prime time for receptivity for a newborn and this initial bonding period immediately after birth should not, unless complications prevent, be missed. During this bonding triangle, talk to your baby, touch your baby, and simply let your emotions go: "Hi baby, this is your father ..." Talk to your baby very much like you did prenatally, using similar words and tone of voice. (See Key 1, Fathering the Pre-born Baby.)

18

6

FATHER BONDING IN A CAESAREAN DELIVERY

D ads, remember, although a caesarean delivery is an operation, it is still a birth. Because of the operation, the mother's bonding with her newborn may be delayed temporarily. But you can help. If medically possible, your wife may request a regional anesthesia (meaning an epidural anesthesia in which your wife is anesthetized from below the level of the navel). Unlike a general anesthesia, which puts the mother to sleep during the operation, the regional anesthesia allows her to be awake and often see her baby born through a mirror, and allows you to see your baby being born. Nearly all hospitals encourage fathers to be present at a caesarean section and to sit at the head of the table holding their wife's hand during the operation. At the moment of birth, the father is able to look over the drape and see the baby lifted up and out. After the caesarean delivered baby is taken care of by attending personnel (usually the baby is put immediately underneath a warmer and given a bit of oxygen if necessary and some of the retained mucous is suctioned) and as soon as "all systems are go" (medical jargon meaning that the baby is active and breathing normally), request that the baby be brought over and placed in your wife's arms on the operating table. Because your wife may be a bit woozy from the sedative and somewhat immobile, you will have to hold your baby next to your wife's face and breasts. This is bonding after caesarean delivery. Perhaps not as comfortable as sitting up in bed, but it is still family bonding time.

While the surgeons complete the operation, go with your baby to the nursery and begin father bonding time. After the operation is finished, and your wife is in the recovery room, you can hold your baby in the nursery, rock your baby, talk and sing and stroke your baby—father bonding at its best. Fathers who get their hands on their babies and take an active role in their baby's care find it easier to get hooked on their babies later on.

Here is a story about a patient of mine who recently had a caesarean birth. I met with this couple prenatally and the mother shared with me that she had difficulty getting her husband, Jim, involved in the pregnancy and feared that he was not going to be involved in the birth. (She expected that he probably would be one of those dads who would become involved as soon as the child is old enough to throw a football.) Jim thought this whole scene of delivering babies was strictly a woman's thing and that he would wait in the waiting room. As it turned out, Mary needed a caesarean delivery, and Jim, the reluctant father, was needed to accompany her into the operating room during the delivery. After the baby was born and I had performed my pediatrician's duties, I asked Jim to accompany me to the nursery.

As soon as we arrived at the nursery, I told Jim that I had to rush to another delivery and that we needed him to help take care of the baby. I impressed upon him that babies breathe better when stroked. I asked Jim to stand next to the infant warmer and stroke his baby, and sing to his baby, and talk to his baby. He looked around to be sure none of his cronies were watching and agreed to do these motherly things. I returned about a half hour later and saw big Jim standing there singing to and stroking his baby as if the pair were really getting to know each other. I mentioned to Jim that he would be surprised at how this initial bonding was going to pay off in the long run. The next day when I made my hospital rounds and went in to talk to Jim's wife, she exclaimed, "What on earth happened to my husband? I can't get our baby away from him. He's really hooked. He would breastfeed if he could. I never thought I'd see that guy be so sensitive."

In a study, reported in *The Role of the Father in Child Development*, M. E. Lamb, Ed., John Wiley, 1981, comparing father involvement in caesarean and vaginally delivered babies, it was found that six months later the fathers of the caesarean delivered babies were more involved in the care giving and soothing activities for their babies. The researchers conclude that this is because fathers, of necessity, were the ones who initially bonded with their babies and were involved very early on with their newborn's care. Bonding with your newborn does, indeed, pay long-term dividends.

7

~~~~~~

MOTHER-INFANT ATTACHMENT—HOW FATHERS CAN HELP

A father is often uncomfortable with a tiny baby and may be equally uncomfortable caring for the mother. A newborn has two basic needs: food and comfort. Most fathers feel unable to meet either of these needs. If your wife is breastfeeding, it is true you cannot provide food, but you can "feed" the mother so that she can better feed your baby. Also, although mothers do have more natural comforting techniques, they do not have an exclusive patent on calming a fussy baby. Fathers can learn to become nurturers too. In this Key, I will focus on teaching new fathers how to begin the care and feeding of their wife during the newborn period. In a subsequent Key, I will discuss how you can become a sensitive nurturer.

John, a new father, described his role for a newborn as, "I can't nurse our baby and I don't always have the means to comfort her, but at least I can create a supportive environment, which encourages my wife to nurse and comfort our baby better." Fathers may have a tougher job during the newborn period than mothers. Fathers have two jobs: caring for their babies directly, and indirectly caring for their babies by taking good care of the mother.

Creating a supportive environment during the newborn period begins with understanding how a mother and baby become attached. This attachment begins before birth. During the nine months of pregnancy, baby and mother develop a natural feeling of oneness. After all, both persons are contained inside one body. But because mothers cannot see their babies in the womb, many mothers feel baby is a bit of a stranger. Birth brings a sense of completeness—baby and mother meet face to face. After birth, a mother's feelings about her baby oscillate between oneness and separateness. In some ways, she regards the baby as a separate person, although still feeling the baby is part of herself. Mother and baby are allowed to experience oneness when they need to be one, and separateness when they need to be separate. Both members of this pair feel fulfilled. If mothers or babies are hurried into separation before they are ready or if their energies are diverted from each other, the normal mother-infant attachment is threatened.

However, bonding immediately at birth is not like some magical glue that cements the mother and baby together forever. Bonding simply gives the relationship a head start. After counseling thousands of new parents, I have found that parents need a minimum of two weeks of close contact with their new baby to start building their attachment to the newborn.

Let's examine how the mother and baby begin to form this attachment—with the father creating the supportive environment that allows this attachment to flourish. The mother-infant attachment begins with both members causing changes in the other. Every baby comes endowed with attachment promoting features and behaviors that are designed to promote care giver signals and alert care givers to the baby's needs. These attachment behaviors and features are the round attractive face with penetrating eyes, a vocabulary of cries and coos, soft skin, and the overall cuddliness that babies

23

exude. These features are designed to cause the caregiver to want to pick up and hold the baby a lot. The mother, in turn, is designed with a sort of built-in receiver that picks up the signals of her baby. The role of the father is to make it easier for the baby (the signaler) and the mother (the receiver) to get together.

Baby likes response. Because the baby has learned he will get a predictable response, he is motivated to give more cues. The mother-baby pair begin to be more comfortable with each other and enjoy each other. Meanwhile, the father creates a supportive environment that encourages the mother to breastfeed and spend interactive time with the baby, which encourages this attachment to develop.

Mutual giving leads to mutual sensitivity. Being sensitive is a crucial part of parenting. If I were asked to sum up the causes of parent-child problems in one word, that word would be *insensitivity*. When a baby and mother are in harmony with each other they become sensitive to each other. When one member of this harmonious pair is upset, the other will also be upset. When one feels right, the other is likely to feel right. It naturally follows that a father should do what he can do to keep both feeling right. It is vitally important for fathers to understand and support this intense mother-infant attachment and not feel threatened by it. To understand how this mother-infant attachment progresses, you may regard your baby's gestation as 18 months—nine months inside and nine months outside. Fathers can and should undertake the care and feeding of the mother during both inside and outside phases of the baby's development. The following are specific ways you can help mothers and babies develop this strong attachment in the early months.

24

Prepare the nest. When the mother and baby come home from the hospital or birthing place (or in the case of home birth, immediately after birth), make the nest—your home—as conducive to mothering as possible. Take over the housekeeping, or hire some help if you can afford it. Because of the tremendously high physiological and emotional changes going on in a postpartum mother, you will find her emotions very labile, to say the least. It is a good idea to stroll around the house each day and take inventory of actual and potential problems that may upset the mother—and then take care of these problems. Remember, the mother's unhappy feelings may be transferred to the baby. An acronym for fathers to remember is TIDY: *Take Inventory Daily Yourself.*

Improve your "serve." A patient of mine, Stan, is a professional tennis player. When they were expecting their first baby, Stan really wanted to be involved with his newborn and asked how he could help his wife. Speaking his language, I advised him to "improve your serve." Many fathers are used to being served by their wives. The postpartum period is a time for you to serve your wife. Serve her breakfast in bed. Take a walk with the baby while the mother takes a shower and has some time for herself in the morning, or during a notorious cranky baby, 4:00 to 6:00 P.M. fussy period. Give your wife frequent "I care" messages as you did during her pregnancy; try to make sure that your messages are such that she clearly perceives your meaning. Take over as much of the housework as you can or see that it gets done by someone else. Take the phone off the hook while mother and baby are sleeping and put a "do not disturb" sign on the door.

Guard your wife against negative visitors. Much of your service to your wife during the postpartum period involves guarding the gates against well-meaning, but intrusive visitors that threaten to upset the harmony of the nest. Love for her baby makes a new mother particularly vulnerable to advice that implies that she might not be doing the best thing for her baby. She is vulnerable to any advice that is proclaimed as a way to make her baby behave "better" by any suggestions that her current style of mothering may do harm to the baby. Fend off these purveyors of bad baby advice. Conflicting advice is confusing to even the most confident mother. It plants doubts in the mother's mind and makes her fearful of lasting harmful effects. If you sense that outside advice is upsetting your wife even slightly, put a stop to it, even if the baby raising tips come from your own mother.

Be sensitive. Be aware of your wife's needs. Many new mothers are reluctant to ask for what they need for fear of shattering their image of a perfect mother and appearing weak in the eyes of their husbands. Fathers sometimes have to figure out what mothers need. One mother told me, "I'd have to hit my husband over the head before he'd realize that I'm giving out."

Take charge when your wife wants to do too much. The overwhelming desire to be a good mother sometimes overrules a woman's ability to know her limitations. Many mothers try to keep up with their pre-motherhood activities. They fail to realize that they do not have enough energy to be all things to all people—maintaining the same social, financial, and other commitments they had before giving birth. My wife used to teach childbirth classes. In one of her classes she advised mothers to stay in their nightgowns for at least three weeks after the baby's birth, the nightgown being a signal to everyone that she is still recovering from giving birth and is to be given to, not taken from. It is up to fathers to take charge of the house and be sure that their wives are not saddled with commitments that drain their energy. An exhausted, overcommitted mother is likely to become a victim of postpartum depression or mother burnout.

Care for the siblings. Fathers and preschool children can be especially demanding during the postpartum period. They are accustomed to having mommy all to themselves and may feel threatened by the presence of the new baby. With other little ones in the family, it is even more essential for Dad to take time off from work during the baby's early days and help the older children adjust to the new baby. Here's how. Develop new games, take lots of trips to the playground, get some special toys. Help your child to feel that even though Mom may spend a lot of time with the new baby, *Dad is sure fun to be with.* Leave specific instructions for older siblings to pick up after themselves. Tell them why particular attention to tidiness is so important at this time. (After all, they are future mothers and fathers.) They should learn that the postpartum period is a time when the whole family *gives* to mom. It is a time for all those little (and big) takers to become givers.

Fathers, recognize that many new mothers are insecure about their mothering capabilities. Their intense love for the new baby brings self-doubt: "I want to be a good mother, but will I be? I want to give my baby the best, but I don't know what the best is!" Both the mother and baby are unorganized and are uncertain as to what is expected of them. To a mother, two important persons help resolve this uncertainty—the baby and the father.

8

NOW WE ARE THREE

Remember those romantic dinners for two? Now you are three. A new dad is not prepared for the realistic fact of family life—sharing his wife with their baby. In Key 7 we discussed the real meaning of a mother's attachment. It is very normal for a father to take a while to adjust to having this little third party in the house monopolizing most of his wife's time and energy and feeling left out of the inner circle of mother and baby.

Be prepared for the following scenario: Your baby is a couple months of age and you are longing for some intimate time with your wife, and she with you. You gear the day to get your baby to sleep early, and the baby is finally asleep. The lights are down low, the candlelight dinner is ready, your wife has put on one of your favorite dresses, and just as you are ready to have some quiet time together, who pipes up wanting his mother—your baby! Suddenly, your wife completely forgets about time with you and breaks a speed record rushing to comfort her crying baby. Again you are alone. These are real moments for most families and are best handled with a little bit of patience and a lot of humor.

Here's how you can steal some time with your wife, yet realize that you are now a family of three. When your baby cries and seems to "interrupt" intimate time together, your first impulse may be to get angry. Instead, try to overcome these feelings and quickly go to the baby yourself saying to your wife, "I'll comfort the baby this time, you relax." This reaction shows a bit of maturity on your part and definitely will win points with your wife, as well as teaching your baby that you are a responsive father.

If there are older children in the family, teach them that their mom and dad need time together. In our 24 years of marriage, we have attempted to have a weekly dinner for two. The older children have learned to respect the evening that we want to be together. They will often look after the younger ones and sometimes they will even act as our "waiters." Not only is this time for two beneficial for you and your wife, it also is good modeling for the children. It teaches them that their mom and dad enjoy being alone together.

Travel as a family. For the first year or two, avoid pressuring your wife to "get away alone." Many mothers normally do not feel comfortable leaving their babies for more than a few hours or even for a day at a time until a child is two or three years of age. Much of these attachment feelings depend upon how separation sensitive the child is and the closeness of the mother-baby relationship. Pressuring the mother to separate from her child before she is ready is doomed to fail, and your anticipated romantic getaway may be much less romantic than you planned. You will have much more fun if you learn to travel as a threesome, at least during the early years of your child's life. Babies are babies for a very short time, and you will soon again have those romantic holidays for two—but now you are three.

9

NURTURING SKILLS FOR THE NEW FATHER

In the previous Keys we stressed one of the father's most important roles in the early months: the care and feeding of the mother. By taking good care of the mother so she can take better care of the baby, the father indirectly participates in the care of his newborn. However, this is only part of a father's role. A father can take a more direct role in caring for his baby. With our first three children, Martha was such a good mother that I did not feel it was necessary for me to do much nurturing of our newborns. She did it so well, and I felt that if I could make the environment more comfortable for her to nurture, then this was my main role. With our next four children, I took a more active role in baby care from the moment of birth on—and even before birth. In this Key I would like to share some nurturing tips that I have learned with our last four children. I only wish I had practiced these tips with our first three!

Nurturing skills for the new father. Dads, picture this common scenario that occurs in the majority of new families. A new baby enters the home and the mother spends most of her waking hours (and some of her sleeping hours) nurturing the baby. By repeatedly nurturing her baby, she and the baby get to know each other very well. The mother becomes more adept at nurturing, the baby gives a cue and the mother responds. After the pair rehearse this cue-response dialogue hundreds of times during the early weeks, they become very good at it. When the baby cries, the mother immediately picks up, nurses, and comforts her baby and the baby stops crying. Because the mother has developed such good nurturing skills and the baby has learned to respond easily, the father takes a backseat to this pair. As soon as the baby cries, the father quickly hands the infant to the mother, who nurses and comforts her baby and the baby stops crying. It always seems to work so well for the mother, why should Dad try to comfort his baby? Over the next few months, both baby and mother become closer to each other and the two are in harmony. Dad is involved, mainly as a spectator and support for the mother, rather than in directly taking care of the baby. As a result, Dad does not learn nurturing and comforting skills and the baby does not learn to respond to his father. When the baby cries and Dad tries to comfort him, the baby cries harder, and the father feels more inept at being a baby comforter.

Even when the father does try to comfort his baby, the mother hovers around nearby waiting to rescue the crying baby from the tense father. As the months go by, the mother becomes tired and burned-out because only she can comfort and care for her baby. She is never able to get away from the baby (so she thinks) because "My baby needs me so much and no one else can care for my baby as well as I can." Because the father has not learned nurturing skills, the mother is afraid to release the baby into his care, and the whole family loses: the mother becomes burned-out, the father does not develop nurturing skills, and the baby does not get close to his father.

Fathers, let me share with you a realistic fact of new parent life that I have learned. A new mother has an overwhelming desire to comfort her baby. As soon as her baby cries, her whole biological system is geared toward comforting the baby. She will not let anyone else comfort her baby unless he has first proven worthy and capable of being a baby comforter. In other words, fathers must first prove themselves as a baby comforter, so the mother feels more comfortable releasing the baby to the father. This is difficult because many mothers do not allow the father to learn comforting skills and a vicious cycle occurs. *My advice to new dads is to learn nurturing skills and become an effective nurturer and comforter of your baby as soon as possible in the newborn period so that your wife feels more comfortable releasing the fussy baby into your care.* The following are time-tested nurturing skills that I have learned and practiced with our babies.

Wear your baby. I feel that it is important for your baby to get used to the rhythm of the father's movement. There are many styles of carriers, so you can find the carrier that is best for you. In my experience, fathers shy away from the front packs and those with many straps and buckles. Put your baby in a sling-type carrier and carry your baby as much as you can. I call this *baby wearing*, rather than just carrying your baby, because you can adjust the carrier to fit the contours of your own body and your baby, and develop a carrying position that fits—much like you would wear a piece of clothing. I have spent some of my most enjoyable hours with one of our new babies in the carrier. *Studies have shown that when babies are worn in a carrier, they cry much less.* Wearing your newborn as much as you can in a carrier gets your baby used to your rhythm of walking and the sound of your voice. By wearing your baby a lot you get used to the "feel" of your baby. If the baby is used to being worn by you when he is in a good mood, it will be much easier for you to calm your baby when he is in a fussy mood.

The neck nestle. Years ago I was wondering what would be a uniquely male comforting position for a baby that would not compete with the natural nurturing skills the mother has, such as breastfeeding, but could work almost as well. This is when I discovered the neck nestle. Place the baby in the front cuddle position and lift him up a bit until his head nestles into your neck, and your neck and chin drape over the baby's skull. You will now have found one of the most comforting and calming of holding patterns. In the neck nestle, the father has a slight edge over the mother. Babies hear not only through their ears, but also through the vibrations of their skull bones. By placing the baby's skull against your voice box in the front of your neck, and humming and singing to your baby, the slower, more easily felt vibrations of the lower-pitched male voice often will lull the baby right to sleep. Hum something low pitched, monotonous, and droning such as *"Old Man River."* An added attraction of the neck nestle is that the baby feels the warm air from your nose on his scalp. My children have enjoyed the neck nestle more than any of the other holding patterns.

The warm fuzzy. Another unique male nurturing technique is the warm fuzzy. Lie on the floor or bed and drape the baby skin-to-skin over your bare chest. Place the baby's ear over your heart. Your baby will love the sound of your heartbeat and the rise and fall of your chest during rhythmic respirations. You will find your baby molding to and settling on your chest.

It is important for the baby to get used to his father's body and the father's unique way of handling. It is not better than his mom's, it is not less than his mom's, it is different. *It is this difference that babies love.* The fact of fathers developing different types of nurturing skills is a very important point. I have always felt my children do not love me less than they do Martha; they love me differently. This is why I feel it is unfair for fathers to be portrayed as simply a pinch hitter to step in and take care of the baby only when the mother is not available. Fathers have unique input also.

By practicing the previous nurturing skills and developing others that work for you and your baby, you are well on your way to becoming a baby nurturer. You will be amazed at the strokes you will get from your baby (and from your wife) by becoming a good nurturer and comforter.

When your child is older, you will begin to see much of the payoff from your early nurturing skills. Researchers who have interviewed teenage boys and girls about how effective their fathers were as disciplinarians report that *the best disciplinarians were first good nurturers and then good limit setters* (see Keys 29–32, Father's Role in Discipline). Developing nurturing skills with your baby in the early months is also a wise long-term investment.

Take paternity leave. Everyone knows the importance of an extended maternity leave, but you never hear much talk of the importance of fathers taking time off. If financially possible, take as much time off as possible to get to know your new baby. Spend quality and quantity time with your baby. Remember, nurturing and comforting may not come as naturally to fathers as it does to mothers. Dads just seem to have to work at it more. It is difficult to learn nurturing skills if you have to sandwich them in scheduled blocks of time between jobs. If possible, you owe it to yourself, your wife, and your baby to take at least a week or two off from work after the birth of your baby. This is the time to get hooked on your baby and your baby to get hooked on you.

10

POSTPARTUM DEPRESSION IN MOTHERS AND FATHERS

Most mothers experience some degree of after-baby blues. The most common symptoms are anxiety, fear, loss of appetite, insomnia, extreme fatigue, outbursts of crying, lack of concern with grooming, making mountains out of molehills, withdrawal from social contact, and often a negative attitude toward the husband. Most fathers feel unable to help their wife's postpartum depression because they do not understand the problem; they do not know how to cope with it nor do they know how to alleviate it. Most postpartum depression results in too many changes happening too fast. It is natural that the high of childbirth is followed by a low. Consider all the changes that take place in your wife after childbirth. Her sleep cycles are disturbed. Her body is rapidly returning to a nonpregnant state; she is experiencing tremendous hormonal fluctuations as the levels of pregnancy hormones gradually diminish and the postpartum hormones take over. These physical changes bring changes in moods and feelings. I feel that the most important cause of postpartum depression is exhaustion. Everything is draining on the new mother.

Some mothers experience more severe postpartum depression than others. Here is how to recognize if your wife has certain risk factors for becoming depressed after childbirth and what you can do to lower this risk. The following factors place a woman at great risk for developing postpartum depression:

- Coming from a high-profile career in which she received a lot of strokes and professional recognition, this woman may have difficulty adapting to a status change. She may have ambivalent feelings about leaving a seemingly more interesting job to become "just a mother" (unfortunately the media do not portray full-time mothering as prestigious and rewarding a job as one outside the home).
- Your marriage has been a bit shaky and you have the unrealistic expectation that having a baby will solve your marital problems.
- The birth experience was negative with overwhelming fear, pain, and the type of birth that the mother did not expect.
- Mother and baby separated after birth. The more mother and baby separation during this crucial bonding after birth, the greater the risk of the mother developing postpartum depression.
- Your wife has a previous history of depression or has difficulty coping with multiple stresses.
- A very fussy (high-need) baby may trigger postpartum depression and/or mother burnout.

Besides making an effort to understand postpartum depression, there are ways that fathers can prevent or ease the problem. I am reminded of the question on the television commercial, "How do you spell relief?" In the case of postpartum depression, I would spell relief F-A-T-H-E-R.

Respect the nesting period. During the first few days after childbirth, encourage your wife to room in with your baby. During the first few weeks at home (which I call the fitting in period), create an environment that encourages the mother and baby to be together as much as possible. This allows them to develop the mutual sensitivity and harmony they need. Respect your wife's nesting instinct. Mothers need a period of uninterrupted settling in time with the new baby.

Mother the mother. Your wife needs mothering too. Try to take over or delegate to someone else the many energy draining tasks that take away from the mother's special time with her baby. In many cultures new mothers receive assistance from a doula, another woman who takes over the household chores and frees the new mother to be with her new baby. A husband can be a doula to the new mother. So can friends. If someone asks if there is anything you need, don't turn down the offer; say, "Yes, bring over an evening meal or help me clean house." Encourage your wife to get regular exercise and eat nutritious meals and snacks. Don't just offer this advice, set up the conditions that allow this to occur. Take the baby yourself and advise your wife, "Honey why don't you go out and get some exercise and I will take care of the baby." Also, fix nutritious meals and snacks for your wife as she may feel "I don't have time to eat because my baby needs me so much."

Encourage group therapy for your wife. Zealous new mothers, who devote themselves entirely to their babies, often withdraw completely from social contacts at the very time they need the support of others. The best of mothers, the ones who try to be perfect, are the ones most likely to become burned-out. They give and give and give and don't realize that they themselves are giving out. Point out to your wife that the traditional cultural model for a mother and baby has never put a mother alone in a room with a baby. It has always been mothers and babies sharing their joys and burdens together. Encourage your wife to join a support group early in the postpartum period or even prenatally. Perhaps the best support group to help a new mother through postpartum depression is the La Leche League International. Dads, remember there is a certain amount of inertia that goes with postpartum depression. Make it easy for your wife to attend support group meetings: "Tonight's the La Leche League meeting. I have already ordered a pizza and after we eat I'll drive you to the meeting and pick you up afterwards."

Go shopping. New mothers often expect that they quickly will regain their pre-pregnant figure and be able to immediately wear all their favorite clothes. These unrealistic expectations cause many women to become depressed and frustrated by their still overweight postpartum bodies. In our society, there is so much emphasis on being slim and trim and fashionably dressed that a new mother's self-esteem takes a real plunge when she is unhappy with the way she looks. Take your wife shopping. But be prepared to be patient. Shopping trips, I freely admit, are a low point of parenting. I simply hate to shop. Be prepared to patiently wait as your wife tries on dozens of dresses. For the first time, your wife has to consider her maternal activities in her fashion choices. Tell her how good a certain outfit looks on her.

Give your wife boosts in her self-image. It is important for you as her mate to accept and approve of who she is and how she looks. Nothing boosts a woman's mood more than to hear the man she loves tell her how beautiful she is. I actually have heard some men tell their postpartum wives that they are too fat or too wide in the hips or otherwise unacceptable. They will never know how damaging that can be to a woman's self-esteem. Above all, don't push your wife to lose weight postpartum. It took nine months to put the weight on and it normally takes nine months to take it off. Slow gradual weight loss is healthy.

Give your wife frequent "I care messages." Lend an ear to helping her verbalize what triggers her postpartum depression. Is it a negative childbirth experience in which she feels that she "failed the course," having a birth different from what she prepared and expected? Does she miss her previous job and all the strokes that came with it? Helping your wife verbalize her feelings gives the message that you really want to understand and help. In delving into why your wife feels depressed most of the time, you will find it usually is due to too many changes too fast. She may just be tired. Listen to the symptoms and early warning signs of postpartum depression. Seek help before a simple case of after-baby blues progresses into a full-blown depression and you wind up being both mother and father to your baby while your wife recovers in the hospital. The single most important way that fathers can help decrease postpartum depression may be summed up in one word: *commitment—commitment to your wife as her husband and commitment to your baby as his father.*

Postpartum depression in fathers. Most fathers themselves experience a bit of postpartum letdown. Fathers do not experience the hormonal and physiological changes that mothers do. Their postpartum adjustment problems are mainly due to the increased responsibilities they face and the sudden changes in lifestyle that occur as a result of being a parent. There are emotional, financial, and sexual adjustments to be made. It helps to think of the postpartum period as another season of the marriage—a season in which more adjustments take place in a shorter period of time than at any other point in your life together. Just as the many minor upsets in babies pass with time, the after-baby blues and depression in mothers and fathers also will pass.

11

NIGHTTIME FATHERING

In recent years, because of changing lifestyles, most babies and children get very little fathering during the day. Because of this fact, developing the art of nighttime fathering is even more important for today's families. This is doubly true in two-income households where nighttime may be the only time of the day when the child receives input from both parents.

Develop realistic expectations of how babies sleep. A realistic fact of nighttime life is that babies don't sleep through the night. They are not designed that way. It might be easier for you to cope with the frequent night waking if you understand what actually goes on in a baby's sleep patterns. During the night, both adults and babies move through cycles of light sleep and deep sleep. During light sleep, a baby squirms and grimaces and always seems on the verge of waking up. During deep sleep, the whole body and mind seem to be completely asleep and the sleeper is more difficult to awaken. Babies experience the whole cycle of going from deep sleep to light sleep and back approximately every hour and a half. Around 80 percent of adult sleep is spent in deep sleep, 20 percent in light sleep. This means that during an average eight hours of sleep, adults may spend approximately six hours in deep sleep and two hours in light sleep.

Babies are designed with different sleep cycles. Babies experience a much larger percentage of light sleep (from 50 to 80 percent) and their sleep cycles are shorter, lasting about 60 minutes. There is a vulnerable period for awakening each time a baby passes from one sleep state into another. This means that babies are programmed biologically to wake up more often than adults. This hardly seems fair to tired fathers, but a basic principle I have learned in 20 years of pediatric practice and 24 years of fathering is that *babies do what they do because they are designed that way.* The ability to awaken easily has survival benefits for the baby. In the first few months of life, the babies' needs are greatest and yet their ability to communicate these needs are least. Suppose a sleeping baby was hungry and did not awaken. Suppose he was cold and did not awaken to protest. Suppose a baby's nose was stuffy and he did not awaken to communicate his need for help. Babies have lots of needs, even at night, and therefore are designed biologically to awaken and communicate these needs. Some researchers also believe that the predominance of light sleep in tiny babies has developmental benefits. During light sleep the brain continues to be active, and this activity enhances brain development.

Babies also fall asleep differently than adults. Adults can move quickly into the state of deep sleep without passing through a long period of light sleep. In other words, adults can "crash" rather easily. Infants, on the other hand, pass through a period of light sleep lasting around 20 minutes before they enter a period of transitional sleep followed by deep sleep. This has important implications for nighttime parenting. Babies should be parented to sleep, not just put down to sleep. They should be nursed and gentled through the initial state of light sleep until they are definitely into a deep sleep. Many mothers will tell you that "My baby has to be fully asleep before I can put him down." It is unrealistic to put a tiny baby into a crib, say "night night," turn out the lights, leave the room, and expect the baby to fall asleep on his own and sleep quietly through the night. It is the nature of many fathers to be a bit impatient in getting their baby off to sleep.

If you understand that babies need to be in a state of deep sleep before they are able to settle, it will help you to patiently father your child off to sleep. If you are rocking your baby, you can tell if she is in a deep enough sleep to be put down on the bed without awakening. Signs that the baby is still in the light sleep stage include facial grimaces (sleep grins), fluttering eyelids, clenched fists, and arms drawn up as if she is trying to hold on to you. A baby in deep sleep, who can be put down gently, has quiet eyelids and facial muscles, open hands, a generally loose feeling and arms dangling at her sides—I call this the "limp limb" sign. When fathering your baby to sleep, place her down on the bed and gently pat her back at a rate of about 60 beats per minute. Very gradually slow down the motion and reduce the intensity of the pats until the baby is in a sound sleep. As babies mature they are better able to go from being awake directly into the state of deep sleep. Their sleep cycles become longer and the percentage of deep sleep increases. Babies gradually settle more quickly and sleep longer, but they seldom achieve adult sleep patterns until two years of age.

How to get your baby to sleep—and stay asleep. Now that you are aware that babies should be parented to sleep, not just put to sleep, here are some tips on how fathers can get their baby asleep—and keep their baby asleep. I call these sleep-inducing tips, techniques for "fathering down." During the first year or two, babies prefer being nursed down to sleep at the mother's breast, especially when they have grown accustomed to this beautiful bedtime ritual. Dads simply cannot and should not attempt to compete with this nursing down ritual. When your wife no longer is breastfeeding, it is important for the father to take over this nursing down. Remember, nursing implies comforting, not only breastfeeding. Only mothers can breastfeed; both mothers and fathers can nurse. Even during breastfeeding, I advise fathers to occasionally try to nurse their baby down to sleep using the following suggestions, so that it will be easier to get their baby to sleep if the mother is not available. After weaning, fathers can take over bedtime rituals. It is only fair that if mothers wake the children up in the morning, fathers should have the job of winding them down at night.

Winding down. The nighttime fathering ritual that my babies and I have enjoyed the most is the art of winding down. When your baby is ready to go to sleep (or you are ready for your baby to go to sleep), place your baby in a carrier and walk around with her. Take a walk around the house or around the neighborhood with your baby. As you are walking, watch for the "limp limb" and other signs that your baby is in a state of deep sleep. Lie down on the bed with your baby still in the carrier, slip yourself out, and let the baby continue to sleep using the carrier as a cover. Or, if your baby sleeps in a crib, you can wind baby down into the crib simply by slipping the carrier over your head and placing the baby down into the crib.

Bedtime. Years ago, early bedtimes were the custom. In rural and farm communities where the family worked together all day, the whole family often retired together early at night, or the baby was put to sleep earlier than the rest of the family. Picture the following nighttime nuisance that is so common in the busy lifestyles of today.

Father often leaves for work early in the morning before the baby gets up. He comes home between six and seven o'clock in the evening. Mother gives the baby a nap early in the afternoon so that the baby will be ready for bed early "so my husband and I can have some quiet time together." When Dad comes home between six and seven o'clock he is expected to have "quality time" with the baby who is tired and cranky and winding down from a busy day and is ready for bed. In other words, Dad has the most time with the baby at the very time of the day when the baby's behavior is the worst. As a result, the baby is not fun to play with and Dad begins to suggest an even "earlier bedtime." The father and baby are out of sync.

If you are a victim of this lifestyle, consider the following alternative: Give your baby his nap later in the afternoon, say around 4:00 P.M. When your husband gets home, the baby has been well rested, is in a good mood, and is ready to play. This quality time then becomes real quality. The father then has more time with his baby at night at a time when the baby is most fun to be with and eager to play. The baby is then put down to sleep at a later hour, perhaps around 9:00 P.M. This works much better than the early-to-bed custom in which a tired baby and a tired father are expected to enjoy each other at a time of the day when all they want to do is rest.

A back rub or massage is a very soothing way to father a child to sleep. Using the power of suggestion, tell your child that he is falling asleep as you work your hands down from his head to his feet. Reassure him that you will stay with him until he is asleep. By the time you finish, he will be sleeping.

12

~~~~~~

SLEEPING WITH YOUR BABY

Fathers frequently ask if it is okay to allow children to sleep with them. I feel that wherever all three of you — mother, father, and baby—sleep best is the right arrangement for your family. In my experience, most babies develop the healthiest sleep attitudes when they sleep with their parents in the same bed. I call this arrangement "sharing sleep" rather than the "family bed" because babies and parents share more than just bed space. They also share sleep cycles and probably a lot of as-yet-undiscovered benefits that come from being in close contact with another person at night.

Besides being good for mothers and babies, sharing sleep benefits fathers too. A baby needs to grow up with the awareness of the presence of his or her father. Most fathers do not get enough daytime contact with their babies. Sharing sleep with your baby helps you make up for the closeness that you both miss during the day. Sleeping with the baby gives a busy father extra touch time with his baby. It usually takes fathers longer to get used to sleeping in the same bed with baby than it does mothers. Even veteran fathers have spent many nights on the living room couch during those noisy first weeks or months with the baby. Dads, hang in there! You will get accustomed to your baby's normal nighttime noises and soon will be able to sleep through them. I have interviewed many fathers concerning their feelings of sharing sleep with their babies. The majority of fathers feel a special closeness with their babies because of this sleeping arrangement. Nighttime fathering and sharing sleep allow "I care" messages to come through all night long, without even saying a word.

As a pediatrician, I frequently get phone calls in the middle of the night. The disturbance of my sleep is eased somewhat by gazing at the face of my little sleeping beauty only a few feet away. It is beautiful for a father and baby to awaken and gaze upon each other's face. Martha and I didn't sleep with our first three babies, but we have enjoyed sharing sleep with our last four. The memories of waking up to the happy faces of my babies will always remain vivid. I believe that babies also carry with them the memories of waking up with the presence of their fathers. I suspect that babies who sleep with their fathers will carry this custom into their own fathering in the next generation.

Some babies and parents are too sensitive to each other's presence during the night and do not sleep well in the same bed. *Sleep-sharing does not work for all families.* Some babies do indeed sleep better with a little space between parents and baby. The *side-car* arrangement gives babies and parents individual sleeping spaces that keeps baby close to mother. Remove one side rail of the baby's crib and place the crib adjacent to your bed. Be sure the mattresses are at the same level and fit snugly to each other so that the baby cannot slip and get caught between them.

If you feel you do not sleep well with the baby in your room and choose instead to have the baby sleep in another room, here is a tip that will win points for you from both the mother and baby. When your baby wakes up at night, go and try to comfort your baby in the other room and try to resettle her. If nursing is what she really needs, then bring the baby to her mother so that your wife does not have to get out of bed. Mothers whose husbands answer these nighttime calls boast about their husband's involvement in nighttime parenting. Nighttime fathering seems to earn extra appreciation from mothers, because getting up and tending to the baby at night traditionally has been delegated to women. With our first few children, I always let my wife answer the distress signals because she had the natural nurturing abilities and equipment for baby soothing. With our last three babies, I have come to feel that it may be unwise for babies to learn to associate only the mother with comfort in times of stress. I have begun to respond to our babies' distress signals. Early on they would greet me with disappointment, as if they had expected their mother's soothing voice and warm breast rather than my hairy arms. But the more I attempted to take on the role of baby soother, the more I found that our babies were willing to accept me as a comforter during times of distress. In most instances, however, babies have a strong preference for their mother as the primary soother and comforter, at least during the first six months.

13

~~~~~~

WHEN FATHERS ARE AWAY—LEAVE A BIT OF YOURSELF BEHIND

E ven fathers who are closely attached and strongly involved with their children must be away because of that dreaded four letter word, W-O-R-K. One of the side effects of becoming a strongly attached and involved father is that the deeper the attachment between the father and child, the deeper the feelings of loss when they are apart. If you have been involved and have invested time in your baby, you have created a feeling of rightness between you when you are together. It follows that you both may feel that things are not right when you are apart. A baby who doesn't feel right, does not act right. When I hear a father boast, "My baby doesn't seem bothered when I am away," I regard this as a sign of poor attachment rather than a positive sign of the baby's independence. A baby who is capable of strong attachments is likely to protest when the objects of his attachment go away. When someone is missing, the structure of his whole world changes. Besides the anxiety that children feel, involved fathers also suffer uneasy feelings when they are away.

Depending on your baby's temperament, the protest may be mild or subtle or strong and obvious. Babies' sleep patterns often change when Dad is away. Night waking is more frequent and getting settled again is more difficult during the father's absences. Babies have more fussy periods and younger children may have more tantrums or angry outbursts. Because the whole structure of their world changes, babies' behavior may be less organized mainly in sleeping and eating schedules.

Discipline problems often surface when Dad's away. Toddlers and young children seem to temporarily "forget" the meaning of "no" and "stop," and older children seem to stretch the father imposed limits when they are only mother enforced. High-need or impulsive children of involved fathers are particularly prone to these separation behaviors. If possible, fathers should try to minimize time away from these special children.

Another effect of the father's absence is that Mom acts differently, especially in a home where there is a strong attachment between the parents and child. Baby gets a double whammy! Father is not there, and the baby feels his absence. Mother, in reacting to her husband's absence, may seem "not all there" too. The baby may even change nursing patterns when his dad is away. Some babies may react by nursing all day and all night! Others may refuse the breast, and the mother may experience a temporary decrease in milk production. In a house where the father is a primary limit setter, older children may take advantage of Mom and test the consistency of her discipline.

Two-year-olds seem particularly sensitive to their father's absence. They may experience mood swings, from quiet withdrawal to impulsive belligerence. They may have trouble figuring out what's happening. A mother once shared with me her two-year-old's reaction to a trip her husband took. She and the child drove Daddy to the airport and waved bye-bye as his plane took off. She explained that Daddy would come back soon on the plane. The next day she found her two-year-old standing in the backyard, pointing at a plane in the sky and yelling, "Daddy."

During a three-day trip, I talked to my one-year-old son, Matthew, on the telephone several times. Martha told me that when Matthew heard my voice he would turn and face the front door. She thought his expression reflected anticipation of seeing me and disappointment when he didn't. The opening door must be a symbol of Daddy's return to small children.

Here are some ways to lessen the effects of father-child separation. When you travel, leave a bit of yourself behind. Try the following:

- Leave photographs of yourself. If your baby is still in a crib, leave large black-and-white photographs of yourself pasted on the wall of his crib or nearby the crib if your child is old enough to yank them off.
- Make a tape recording singing and talking to your baby. Use songs and phrases that your baby associates with you.
- Call frequently to talk to your baby or child. Call around bedtime and tell a surprise bedtime story.
- Suggest that your wife tell the children stories about you and your childhood while you're away.
- Consider taking your family or one of your older children with you when you travel. Babies are very portable and travel easily. Home to a tiny baby is where Mom and Dad are, whether it's your house or a distant hotel room. It is also valuable for your child to know what Dad does when he travels. Take him with you to a meeting; let him see you giving a lecture. Let your child see you in situations where you are in the spotlight. I frequently have taken my children with me when I appear on television. It is interesting for

them to see behind the scenes in a father's life. The long plane rides also gives you some one-on-one time with your child that you may not have in a busy home. Taking one child with you when you travel is especially valuable for fathers of large families.

- Don't forget to bring back presents. The custom of bringing presents to your children every time you travel can be fun, but it may be a financial hardship. Airport gift shops are a special weakness to traveling fathers. Because I travel a lot giving talks to parent groups, I frequently would change planes at the Dallas Airport. Over the years, my children seem to have collected a large array of Dallas Cowboy uniforms. My son, Peter, is an avid baseball fan. On each trip I try to find him a different baseball cap. His large collection may remind him that his father is away frequently, but I hope it also reminds him that while I'm away I think of him.

Don't be disturbed if your baby gives you the cold shoulder when you return. This is only temporary. Babies feel a mixture of anger and confusion about separation and require some time to adjust to your return. The first time I experienced this reaction, I was devastated. I walked in the door after being away for several days, I expected to be greeted with some "happy to see you" signs from our one-year-old. Instead, his attitude for the first few hours was more like "I could care less." I picked him up and walked with him, his head nestled into my neck. As I began to sing his favorite song, he perked up. I had struck a familiar note, and we were reunited. Sometimes you have to woo your baby back to trusting you.

14

~~~~~~

TRAVELING TIPS FOR FATHERS WITH CHILDREN

- Be sure to take along a sling-type carrier as this will confine baby in busy airports, gift shops, and while waiting in lines.
- Select the right seat on the airplane. The bulkhead seat has the most legroom, although the armrests are fixed. Some parents find the retractable armrests in all but the bulkhead seats allow for more family closeness. If you and your wife and baby are traveling together, ask for an aisle and window seat. Let the ticket agent know you are traveling with a baby and the airline usually will leave the middle seat open (few people want to sit in the middle between the mother, father, and baby).
- Ask for your meals to be served in shifts. Offer to hold your baby on your lap while your wife eats first.
- Bring along a "bag of tricks," a few of the baby's favorite toys or even some new special toys that are reserved just for traveling. Babies love novelty and quickly become bored with the same old toys.
- It's a vacation for your wife also. This is not a time to sit in your airline seat immersed in a magazine while your wife tends to a squirming baby. When your baby begins to fuss, tell your wife, "Relax, and I'll walk up and down the aisle with our baby."

- Choose lodging that is family oriented and considerate of babies. In selecting a hotel room, remember that tiny babies are predominantly nose breathers and are very sensitive to dry air. It clogs their nasal passages. Avoid the newer hermetically sealed hotel rooms in which the windows do not open. Tiny babies enjoy fresh humid air.

Traveling, whether for vacation or on business, is a time for fathers to really shine. It is a time for you to take over as much of the baby care as you can, give your wife a rest, and really get to know your baby. Travel time affords you the luxury of both quantity and quality time, a combination that both you and your baby greatly need.

15

~~~~~~

THE WORKING FATHER—JUGGLING FATHERHOOD AND CAREER

One of the most difficult tasks for a father is to juggle two careers: fathering and working. Mothers are just beginning to experience the same dual-career dilemma that fathers have endured for centuries. In this Key, I would like to share with you some practical tips for balancing your career at home and in the office.

If possible, do much of your work at home. One of the problems in my life has been achieving a balance between spending time with the children in my home and the children in my pediatric practice. I love them all. I hear so much about mothers feeling guilty when they leave their babies, but it seems to me that fathers get a double dose of this kind of guilt. I feel guilty when I am away from my own children, and I feel guilty when I am away from the children that I am responsible for in my practice. Being available is an important part of being a pediatrician and a father. I didn't realize the importance of the father being home until I experienced a year of being a "home father."

A few years ago, in the midst of building a new office, the lease expired in my old office. This time of transition between offices provided me with an opportunity to increase my availability to my family, although not compromising my availability to my patients. I decided that, for a short time, I would move my office into our home. The idea for this rather unconventional professional setup, came during one of our family discussions in which we "take inventory" of how things are going with everyone. We often play the "if you could change things" game. It's a way of finding out what our children are feeling and imagining, and what changes may be needed. I asked our ten-year-old, Peter, to tell me what he would wish if he could change anything. His response was, "Dad, I wish you could work at home." The whole family helped renovate a large area in our garage that became my temporary pediatric office. My teenage patients called it, "Dr. Bill's garage and body shop." Wanting to be sure that I made a lot of brownie points with my children, I let them know that I was moving my office into our home so that I could be closer to them. I did impress upon them that this office was primarily for my work, and that while I was there I would be working, not playing.

What a revelation! I realized that traveling to my job every day may have been exhausting, but it was also a therapeutic escape. Initially, I missed the camaraderie of the office building—the mutual stroking and recognition that goes on between colleagues in elevators and hallways or during coffee or lunch breaks. Now, with my office at home, when I wasn't with my patients, my social world was just my family. Even though I could escape into my garage, I had to relate to my family all day long and I was not accustomed to this. Having my office in my home opened my eyes to another unfortunate effect of social change in our industrial society. When fathers are forced to leave their homes for the marketplace, they lose the ability to relate to their families on a day-to-day basis. They become more comfortable with the social interactions of their workplace. Most fathers get more strokes at their office than they do at home. Children are not noted for exuding appreciation for their parents. This experience also helped me understand why a former career woman often feels isolated when she becomes a full-time mother and stays home with the baby all day long. My year at home in Dr. Bill's garage turned out to be the most memorable of my 24 years of fathering. I knew my children much better during that year, and they knew me because they were accessible to me and I was accessible to them. I witnessed our one-year-old, Matthew, take his first step, and I was available during certain high-need periods when our children simply needed to check in with me for a few seconds—and they often did between patient appointments. Our children may not remember my year at home, but I shall never forget!

If possible, incorporate your children into your work life instead of maintaining a strict separation of job and family. Take your child into your office with you especially if you have to work an occasional weekend or after hours. If you have an interesting business meeting where you will be performing or topics will be discussed that are of interest to your child, take your child with you. Give your children summer and holiday jobs in your office.

Modeling your work for your child is especially important if you would like them to consider following in your footsteps. By incorporating your child into your work, he or she is able to understand your career. I frequently took our two oldest boys on hospital rounds with me. It paid off; during the writing of this book, I helped them both fill out applications to medical school!

What is the result of frequent father absence from the home? I have surveyed the literature on the effect of father absence and discovered the following: Although both boys and girls are affected, father absence seems to have more of an effect on boys than girls. In one study, boys were found to have more difficulty in assuming masculine roles when they were separated from their fathers in early childhood. Boys seemed to be particularly vulnerable to the father's absence during early developmental stages when they are learning to control their own impulses. Boys between the ages of twelve and thirty months show more aggressive behavior when their fathers are absent. Researchers believe that young boys need a father at particular stages of personality development to help them control their inborn masculine aggressive tendencies. Sleep disturbances, such as nightmares and fears, are often common when fathers are gone. Boys experience *father hunger—some inner fear threatens to overwhelm them and leads to a specific longing for the father.*

Girls reared in homes where the father is absent show a higher incidence of difficulties in later interactions with males. Boys from homes where their fathers were absent were described by their teachers as less advanced in moral development. Studies have also shown that mothers without husbands have more power over their children because they are required to be the "heavy" in discipline disputes. However, children of absent fathers tend to respond less to the mother's disciplinary measures. Having a father around who will back up the mother's decisions gives her credibility and increases the likelihood that the child will respect her discipline. Fathers have their own unique contribution to make to infant development as do infants on their father's development. When the father is absent, neither the baby nor the father develop as well.

It is important for your child to know where your priorities are. Even though you may need to work away from home, your child should understand that your home is more important. Being absent by necessity is pardonable; being absent by choice is not. Fathering is indeed an "at home job."

16

IS THERE SEX AFTER CHILDBIRTH?

Most fathers feel that they suffer from an acute lack of sex in the first few months after childbirth. Fathers whom I have interviewed on this subject relate, "I feel left out." "I've got needs too." "We need to get away—alone." "We haven't made love for weeks." Let me assure you that these feelings and your wife's strong attachment to your baby are both very normal.

Your wife's sexual desires are different after childbirth. By understanding the hormonal changes that take place in your wife after childbirth, and recognizing the importance of the mother-infant attachment, it might be easier for you to understand your wife's apparent lack of interest in sex. A woman has two sets of hormones, sexual hormones and maternal hormones. Prior to childbirth, the hormones to be a mate, the sexual hormones, are higher than the hormones to be a mother. After childbirth, the reverse occurs, the maternal hormones are higher than the sexual hormones. This hormonal reversal may last until the baby is weaned. During this time, your wife's desire to take care of or nurse your baby may take priority over her desire for sexual intimacy with you.

A season of the marriage. As a survivor of my wife's hormonal changes through many children, I have developed a theory as to why these changes occur. During my years as a pediatrician and as a father I have learned that not only do babies do what they do because they are designed that way, but mothers also do what they do because they are designed that way. The shift from attachment to the husband to attachment to the baby seems to be a normal design for the survival of the species. This assures that the young of the species are well mothered. I explained this all one day to a left out new father. He commented, "This seems to be part of the for-better-or-for-worse clause in the marriage vows: better for the baby, worse for the daddy."

Another reason for your wife's apparent sexual uninterest is she is fatigued. Mothers often feel so drained by the consistent demands of the baby and household that at bedtime all they want to do is to sleep. Mothers whom I have interviewed on this subject have described this end-of-the-day feeling as being "all touched out" or "all used up." These feelings are especially prevalent if you have a high-need baby. A mother is programmed to be attached to your baby physically, chemically, and emotionally. This does not mean that you are being displaced by the baby, but that some of the energies previously directed toward you are now being directed toward your baby. For the first months after childbirth (sometimes longer), most wives do not have the energy to engage in a high level of intimacy both as a mother and as a sexual partner. One tired mother, who was trying to define the difference between needs and wants, told me, "My baby needs nurturing; my husband wants sex." Dads, don't feel that your wife deliberately cuts you off.

Meanwhile, you can do something to build up your equity in your wife's sexual interest in you: If you become a supportive and sensitive husband during this early attachment period in the first few months, your wife's love and respect for you will grow and her interest in you will return at a higher level. I call this early attachment period a *season of the marriage,* a time to parent. If you carefully nurture the harvest of this season, the season to be sexual will follow and will be richer. Here's how to rekindle the sexual fire after childbirth.

Don't pressure your wife into sex. Pregnancy, birth, and the early postpartum adjustment period leave a woman physically and emotionally drained. Let your wife's whole system settle down a while before hinting at sexual demands. As most husbands know, the mental components of sex are much more important in women than in men. In women, physical and emotional readiness for sex occur together. This is especially true during the postpartum period. A woman's mind usually is not ready for sex until her body is. Many women truly are not ready for sexual intercourse for several months after birth. Pressuring your wife to give too much too soon is doomed to failure. Sex given out of a sense of obligation is not as good as sex motivated by desire.

Go easy. Respect the physical changes that are going on as your wife's body returns to its pre-pregnancy state. Some fathers have described their sexual reunion with their wives as "getting to know her body all over again." Sensitivity and gentleness are the keys to fulfilling postpartum sex. Your wife's breasts may be sensitive because of the changes that occur during lactation. They may leak milk while you're making love, so be prepared for this with a towel nearby to catch the drips. Your wife may also experience vaginal discomfort or pain during intercourse. The hormones that usually prepare the vagina for intercourse by releasing a protective lubricant are at a lower level during lactation, making vaginal dryness very common in the months after birth. Vaginal pain may also occur if your wife had an episiotomy that has not yet been healed completely. Here are some suggestions to help you and your wife get reacquainted sexually:

- Make the first night you plan to have intercourse after the birth similar to your first experience with intercourse together—a special time of romance and courtship, complete with flowers and a special dinner. With all the recent changes in your wife's body, you will be getting to know each other all over again. One plus is that "the bulge" is gone, and you will be able to snuggle close together again.
- Experiment with positions that do not put pressure on your wife's breasts or episiotomy, for example, the side-to-side position. Move slowly and ask her to guide your penetration to avoid pain.
- If dryness is a problem, use a water-soluble lubricant.
- Leaking breast milk is a natural part of sex after childbirth. Don't give your wife the message that this normal body function is distasteful. If leaking milk bothers you, having sex after the baby has emptied the breasts may lessen the problem. Understand this process for what it is: a sign that your wife's body is responding to your lovemaking.

Respect your wife's mother-infant attachment. The feeling of oneness between a mother and her new baby may affect your lovemaking. You may often feel that you are making love to a split personality; your wife's body may be in your arms, but her mind may be with her baby. Picture this scenario: While you and your wife are making love, your baby cries from another room. When this happens, your wife's body and mind respond and she will be more oriented toward comforting baby than satisfying Daddy. Fathers, it is impossible to compete with this normal biological programming. Above all, avoid giving your wife the feeling that your baby is spoiling your sexual pleasure. Instead of letting loose with an angry "foiled again" reaction, be sensitive to your wife's biology and to your baby's needs. Say to her, "Go comfort the baby first, and we'll make love later." Nothing will earn you more points (and better sex!) than to convey to your wife your understanding that the baby's needs come before yours. A woman is often turned off by selfishness in a man, particularly when it comes to sex. But she will return to your side feeling even more loving and responsive if you have encouraged her to meet the baby's needs first. *Although you may feel deprived, telling your wife, in words or actions, that the baby has had enough of her attention and that "now it's my turn" is a guaranteed turnoff.*

Sexual understanding leads to sexual maturity. An important part of becoming a mature person is being able to give a part of yourself to someone else. Another part of growing up is learning to delay your own desires in order to answer a need that someone else has. New fathers go through a kind of second adolescence. Adolescents are naturally impulsive but must learn it is often wise to delay gratification of their impulses. You may feel that you want to get away alone with your wife and that the baby always wants her when you want her. You realize that you must share your mate with another person. Handling these feelings can have a maturing effect on a man. Remember, during the first year, most of what a baby demands from parents is simply what he or she needs. Resenting your baby for taking your wife away from you or resenting your wife for putting the baby's needs first can stand in the way of becoming a giving father. It can also greatly diminish the joys of being a parent. *Fatherhood is one big give-a-thon.* The earlier we learn to give, the greater the joy in becoming a father.

Fathers who have felt that they are suffering from an acute lack of sex in the first few months after childbirth but have developed the maturity to accept delayed gratification of their needs, often find that their overall relationship with their mate improves. Understanding and respecting the natural design of the first few months after childbirth forces the husband to seek ways of achieving sexual intimacy with his wife outside of intercourse.

In ancient times, writers about sex described the sexual relationship as "to know" another person. Whereas this can be interpreted specifically to mean sexual intercourse, I believe the phrase "to know" conveys many other levels of meaning. It describes the mutual adjustments that a couple make when they become parents. By understanding that a sexual relationship involves more than intercourse, the husband truly gets to know his wife. Yes, dads, there is sex after childbirth! It is a fuller, richer kind of sex that matures a man as a male person, a husband, and a father.

17

FATHERING THE
FUSSY BABY

Some babies come wired with needs that require a high level of parenting. You can often spot these babies as newborns. It is as if, right after birth, they look up and say, "Hi Mom and Dad. You've been blessed with an above average baby, and I need above average parenting. If you give it to me, we're going to get along fine; if you don't, we're going to have a bit of trouble down the road." Early on, these babies receive a variety of labels: fussy, demanding, difficult, exhausting, colicky, hyperactive; the list goes on. None of these terms really describes what these babies are like, and the style of parenting they need. I prefer to call this special kind of child the "high-need child." This is not only a kinder term, but it is more accurate. It describes what these children are like and suggests something about the kind of parenting they need.

High-need babies can put a severe strain on families if their needs are not recognized and responded to sympathetically. They require a great deal of parenting energy, but the investment-return ratio is high. The more you give to this type of child, the more you and the rest of the family will get back in return. In looking over my gallery of parents who have survived and thrive with their high-need baby, one important highlight stands out—*a sensitive and involved father.* "I could not have survived without the help of my husband," confided Mary, a tired but fulfilled mother of a high-need baby.

Having an involved father and sharing the parenting is a desire in most families. For high-need babies, it's a must.

How to recognize the high-need baby. The following are the most common personality traits that parents use to describe their high-need baby:
- supersensitive
- intense, hyperactive, hypertonic
- "I can't put him down"
- draining
- awakens frequently
- unpredictable
- uncuddly
- "wants to nurse all the time"
- demanding

These traits of a high-need baby may sound predominantly negative. This is how parents perceive these babies early on. I have observed, however, that sensitive parenting can turn these seemingly negative traits into more positive ones. Parents gradually begin to describe their high-need children in more positive ways: interesting, challenging, and bright. In this Key, I wish to help fathers turn these difficult qualities into creative assets. Fathers have an important role to play in parenting their high-need child. They can help in three ways: by interacting with the baby, by supporting the mother, and by improving their own sensitivity.

The need-level concept. It may help you to further understand the profile of a high-need baby by understanding that some babies behave the way they do because of their own temperament. Every baby has a distinct temperament that is genetically determined. By temperament I mean the way the child behaves, how he communicates, how he reacts to the world around him—his style. Babies also have different levels of needs and they come wired with a corresponding temperament to alert their care givers of this level of need. Babies have an intense desire to fit into their environment, and they will use their personality traits to alert their care givers to their level of needs in order to help them fit.

High-need babies have a hard time fitting in. They need lots of care and attention from parents to help them fit. Fortunately, they come endowed with temperaments that ensure that they get the attention they need.

A baby who needs to be held a lot in order to fit into his environment, for example, will cry intensely until he is picked up and will start crying again when he is put down. Babies don't cry in order to annoy, manipulate, or make their parents miserable. They cry to communicate their needs.

Babies with greater needs give more intense cues. This is why high-need babies are often labeled as "demanding." Being demanding is a positive character trait that helps baby reach his or her maximum developmental potential. Consider what would happen if a high-need baby were not demanding. If this particular baby needed to be held a lot in order to reach his full potential, yet did not have the corresponding temperament to alert his care givers, he would not receive the help he needs to fit into his environment. His developmental potential would be threatened because he would not learn to trust his own cues or the people around him. This baby, if he were not demanding, may not develop a sense of confidence and self-esteem. Babies do what they do because they are designed that way. Respecting that design ensures that the baby will develop his full potential and so will the parent.

Another part of the need-level concept is how the baby's temperament affects the parents. Every baby comes endowed with a certain level of needs and a corresponding temperament to communicate these needs to his parents. Every parent is endowed with a certain level of giving. The demanding level of the baby and the giving level of the parent begin to match; the parents and baby fit together. The family fits together. Family harmony occurs. In counseling many parents of high-need babies, I have seen that one of the beautiful aspects is how the baby also develops the parent. Because these babies have a way of extracting creative parenting techniques from you, you will find that after years of parenting a high-need baby (although exhausted), you will have developed skills that you never had before. How you father your high-need baby affects two people: your baby and your baby's mother. Your wife needs your psychological support and your readiness to fill in as "the mother" when she runs out of steam. In parenting the high-need baby, the mother-father roles are not so well defined. The following tips are geared to help the father and his high-need baby bring out the best in each other. High-need babies are discussed in Barron's *Keys To Calming The Fussy Baby*.

18

CO-PARENTING THE FUSSY BABY

There will be times when you are down too, especially if your baby has been crying a lot during the night or you are frustrated at your inabilities to comfort your baby. Try to keep your wife from sensing that you have negative feelings about your baby's behavior because this reinforces her feelings that the baby's behavior is her fault.

By disapproving of your baby, you also are giving your wife the message that you disapprove of her mothering and, therefore, of her. Many mothers derive a lot of their self-esteem from how their husbands perceive their mothering abilities. We all need strokes, especially mothers and fathers of high-need babies.

Here are some suggestions to support your wife in co-parenting the fussy baby:

Encourage your wife to seek outside support. Surround yourselves with supportive friends. Nothing divides people like differing parenting styles. Protect your wife from these negative advisors by purposely seeking out friends who share your own parenting style and who can be supportive of you rather than critical.

Get help at home. It is not so much the incessant needs of high-need babies that drive mothers to the edge, it is the energy demands from trying to be all things to all people. Avoid making demands on your wife to be a hostess, gourmet cook, housekeeper, and so on. Give her the message, "You're doing the most important job in the world, mothering our high-need baby. I don't expect you to do anything else at this stage in our baby's life; I'll take over all the other stuff." Hire help at home or pitch in yourself to free your wife of non-mothering chores that divert her energy away from baby, and also away from you.

Be involved. The mother-father roles are not so well defined with high-need babies. Shared parenting is not only desirable for the high-need baby, it is absolutely necessary. Take over when times get tough. Fussy babies usually save their most exhausting behavior for the end of the day, between 4:00 and 6:00 P.M., when the mother's energy reserves are lowest. Some parents humorously call this the "happy hour." If you come home from work at the end of the day, and your castle, queen, and little princess are all a wreck, it's not a good time to express your disappointment. Instead, say to your wife, "You take a nap and do something just for yourself, and I'll take over with the baby." Here are some creative father comforting techniques you can try when you do take over care of your baby.

Freeway fathering. Secure your baby safely in a car seat and take a nonstop ride for at least 20 minutes. Fussy babies often quiet down during a ride. When you return home and the baby is in a deep sleep, don't risk waking him by removing him from the seat. Instead, carry the baby with the car seat and all into the house to continue his nap.

Wear your baby. Put your baby in a carrier and take a walk around the neighborhood. See Keys 9 and 11 for suggestions on different holding patterns that help the fussy baby settle.

Give your wife a break today. There may be times when your baby simply wants and needs to be put down on a soft carpet and allowed to blow off steam. Sometimes fathers are better at recognizing these times than mothers. Your wife's natural reactions to the baby's signs of distress are either holding or nursing, and most of the time these do the job. However, sometimes it takes a suggestion from the father to find a way to calm a fussy baby: "Maybe she needs some exercise to blow off a little steam. I'll sit here with her for awhile so you can take a break." Some mothers simply need permission to detach from their baby. *When you offer advice to your wife about baby care, focus on what you feel the baby needs at that moment, not on what you feel your wife ought to be doing.* Remember that your wife often feels that her baby is acting the way she does because of something she is doing wrong.

Avoid escape fathering. Fathering a high-need child often reminds me of the advice that the famous Notre Dame football coach Knute Rockne gave to his players, "When the going gets tough, the tough get going." In other words, tough guys hang in there rather than trying to escape. Your wife may feel that you are frustrated at your apparent lack of success in always comforting your fussy baby. This may prompt you to withdraw from the care of your baby altogether and "wait until this stage passes" and then reenter as a father. In this situation everyone loses—your wife, your baby, and you.

19

∿∿

THE QUALITY TIME MYTH

One difference I have noticed in the way that mothers and fathers care for babies is that fathers seem to like to schedule and structure the play time, whereas mothers usually go with the flow of the baby's mood. This is the main problem with the quality time myth. You may be in the mood to play with your baby, but your baby may want to sleep or just be cuddled. Babies are very mood dependent in their desire to play. If you have work to do at home, but are minding the store, it is easier to schedule your work around the baby's down times rather than to try to structure the baby's time around your work. Watch for the state of "quiet alertness"—that prime time of receptivity when the baby is most in the mood to play. Babies in this state have wide open eyes and are relatively quiet, not wriggling or fussy. Babies are most attentive during this time and their otherwise very limited attention span is longer.

Develop dad games. Plan special play activities for the times when you and your baby are alone. Choose activities that are different from how the two of you play together when Mom's around. This makes it easier for the baby to accept your care, especially during the first year when babies are very sensitive to the mother's absence.

Care for the baby during prime time. Sometimes fathers only take care of their baby when the mother is worn out or the baby is particularly fussy. I recommend that the father insist on taking over regularly, and not wait until the mother has had it. (This is discussed further in Key 21, Helping Your Wife Avoid Burnout.) By taking over I mean as completely and for as long as possible. After the child is weaned, it could be for a whole day. Encourage your wife to take an occasional day off and leave your baby with you. She will love you for it, and will run out of physical and emotional energy far less frequently. There should be no possibilities for the father to bail out. Let the mother enjoy a whole day of creature comforts and not have to worry about her baby. An hour, a morning, or a day of peace is wonderful, and does wonders to renew your wife's energy in her baby, and you. A father will never know his child fully until he has sole responsibility for decision making: Does he need a diaper change? Is she hungry? Does he need to cuddle? Is she cold? Becoming sensitive to your child's signals depends upon your desire to do so. You cannot perfect your cooking skills by watching someone else cook. You'll never perfect your parenting ability while watching your wife parent. Having full responsibility for my children has been one of the most rewarding and enjoyable experiences of my life. Father and children invariably will grow closer, as they become more aware of and sensitive to each other's feelings. Also, the father and mother will both find comfort in knowing that in the event of emergencies, the father can confidently and effectively care for the children. This is an all-win situation—for father, mother, and children.

Be safety minded. Accidents may occur more readily when the father is minding the store. I do not mean to imply that fathers are careless, but they may not be completely aware of babies' compulsive behaviors and capabilities at a given stage of development. Sometimes I wonder if mothers really do have eyes in the backs of their heads, along with third arms and radar systems that pick up on babies' collissions with furniture before they occur. Fathers need to be aware that because they are new to the job of safety patrolling, they need to be extra cautious in leaving the baby unattended. You may be very tired, but resist the urge to take a nap while solo fathering. Mothers seem to have a heightened awareness of their babies even during sleep, but fathers usually don't. Although this ability to tune out babies' cries can be an asset during nighttime co-parenting, it is a liability during solo fathering.

Be consistent. It is unimportant that you respond to your baby's cries in the same way your wife does; after all, you are not the same person. It is important for your baby to develop trust in you. He should know that his cues will be responded to, that when he cries, he will be comforted. It is important to your baby's self-esteem that he gets the response he has learned to anticipate. For example, a baby who has learned to trust his parents expects that distress will be followed by comfort. Your method of comforting the crying baby may be different from your wife's, but it is important that you respond to your baby's cry. A time when you are solo fathering is not the time to "let the baby cry it out." This is not likely to make a baby look forward to those times alone with you.

20

~~~~~~

DIAPER CHANGING
TIPS FOR DADS

Babies probably don't like wearing diapers any more than fathers like changing them. But, like many of the nuisance baby stages, this too shall pass. Until it does, here are some tips that will cut down on the hassles of changing your baby's diapers.

Health and safety tips. Falling off changing tables is probably the most common accident that occurs during diaper changing. It takes a baby just one millisecond to roll off a counter or a changing table while your back is turned or you are searching for a diaper or pin. Most changing tables have a safety strap across them. Be sure to use it. Pin safety is also important. Don't leave open pins within grabbing distance of your baby. Don't hold diaper pins in your mouth; your baby may imitate this dangerous habit. For fathers who are not used to changing table safety, it is safest to use the floor. Because babies usually associate the floor with rolling, expect more of a wrestling match with your baby when trying to get him to lie still on his back on the floor. Sometimes a baby associates the changing table with lying still and may squirm less. Change your baby's diapers frequently, especially if she is prone to diaper rash. The super absorbent diapers are especially difficult to tell when wet. When a wet diaper is on the baby too long, it will irritate her sensitive skin.

I feel that diaper pins are part of a subversive plot devised by mothers against husbands. I don't like them and they don't like me. You could "cheat" and use disposable diapers with plastic adhesive tape. If your baby is allergic to plastic diapers or you are mindful of the ecology, save disposable diapers for traveling and use cotton diapers at home. Instead of pins, use cloth diaper covers with velcro fasteners.

One of the biggest hassles of diaper changing is the combination of the wiggly infant and the impatient father. Most of the time, diaper changing amounts to a wrestling match of a grown man trying to corral a wiggly and rolling baby. Here's how to keep your baby quiet during diaper changing. Use a "settling event"—a pattern of pleasant behavior that the baby can associate with diaper changing that will put him in a more receptive mood. Reserve one of your baby's favorite songs for diaper changing and begin singing this right before the change. When your baby hears his favorite song he is more likely to quiet out of interest in the pleasing event that will soon follow. At times, dangling a special toy from your mouth, your third hand, during changing will settle the squirming baby. Again, reserve this toy only for diaper changing. Sometimes a dangling mobile that is fixed above the usual diaper changing area will hold the baby's attention. A little game that our babies have enjoyed is walking your fingers up and down their legs and abdomen during the change while singing a song.

Make funny faces during the diaper changes. Reserve special funny facial gestures and contortions to interest your baby during this wrestling match. Your baby will focus on your face rather than on what you are doing to clean up his bottom. Diaper changing is a social event, a time when fathers and babies share feelings. The baby senses that the father, fumbling though he may be, cares about his bodily needs; fathers, in turn, often sense that their babies appreciate their efforts.

Be creative. With an older baby you may need to go through great lengths to distract attention away from the diaper changing activity. What worked best for me was changing our one-year-old son Matthew's diapers on a skateboard. The skateboard is one of his favorite toys, and he loves to push it along the floor. In his mind, anything associated with the skateboard must be all right. The only way I can get him to hold still during a diaper change is to place him on a covered skateboard.

One final tip. Beware of your male baby suddenly becoming quiet after wiggling. He probably is preparing to squirt you.

21

HELPING YOUR WIFE
AVOID BURNOUT

In Key 10 we discussed postpartum depression and saw how a burned-out mother is also a burned-out wife. In this Key, I'll give you help to prevent this common disease of modern mothers as quickly as you can. Burnout is usually a result of a dedicated mother trying to do too much for too many with too little help. A misconception about burnout is that it occurs only in a weak mother. Not true. Burnout is a disease of the strong, not the weak and it is most common in mothers who are committed to becoming the perfect mother. A mother has to be on fire first before she can burn out!

How to recognize the early signs of burnout. Fathers are notorious for their inability to recognize when a mother is at the end of her rope, and mothers are noted for their untiring energy and unwillingness to ask for help before they burn out. Mothers do not want to appear weak in the eyes of their husbands. Therefore, even if they recognize early symptoms of burnout in themselves, they may fail to share these symptoms with their husbands. It is up to you as a father to recognize the symptoms of impending burnout.

There are two categories of risk factors predisposing burnout: a high-need baby and a certain type of mother. Mothers of high-need babies run a higher risk of burning out. Babies have a way of extracting large amounts of energy from their mothers. Mothers, in turn, are programmed to be giving and nurturing and to supply all the energy demanded by the baby. This is nature's way of ensuring the survival of the young of the species. Mothers keep giving and babies keep taking, sometimes to the point where mothers lose touch with their own needs and fail to realize that they are burning out. The mother is programmed to fill her baby's needs, but who takes care of the mother's needs? That's where the father comes in. As we discussed earlier, in a family with a high-need child, fathers must help balance the needs equation. They do this by giving to both the mother and baby and by helping the mother realize her own limitations.

Besides certain types of babies predisposing the mother to burnout, the following are factors that may increase a woman's risk of burning out:
• highly motivated and compulsive mothers;
• mothers of babies who are close in age—fewer than two years apart;
• women who are involved in high-profile careers who become full-time mothers;
• women who experience a stressful labor and delivery or who were separated from their babies after birth because of medical problems;
• the busy nest syndrome: moving, remodeling, attending to too many visitors and social commitments; and
• mothers experiencing marital discord, especially those who unrealistically believe that a baby will solve the problems of the marriage.

Signs and symptoms of burnout. One of the earlier signs of burnout is when your wife begins to feel she is not a good mother. She may stop taking care of herself and pay less attention to her grooming, unknowingly making herself less attractive to you. She may excuse this by saying, "My baby needs me, I don't have time for anything else." What energy she has goes to the baby, with little left over for herself and none at all left over for you. Mothers nearing burnout tend to make mountains out of molehills. They are confused by the slightest setback and tend to jump all over their husbands with very little provocation. A messy kitchen or an untidy living room may set off a wave of depression, and sometimes even one dirty dish can trigger a weeping spell.

Burned-out mothers suffer from inertia. They quit exercising and have trouble getting going for any activity except sitting and nursing their baby. Burned-out mothers also suffer from insomnia, part of the underlying depression that creeps into a mother. Mothers of demanding babies actually need more sleep, but they seldom get it.

Dads, don't be surprised if you have a hard time convincing your wife that she is burning out. This takes tact and diplomacy. Here is an angle that has worked many times for me: *Don't preach.* Instead of focusing on what's best for the mother or on your unmet needs, *focus on what's best for the baby.* Few mothers can resist this approach.

Mothers naturally respond to the what's-best-for-the-baby approach because they have programmed themselves to think of the baby first. Convince your wife that taking better care of herself will benefit the baby.

Some mothers actually need permission to release themselves temporarily from their obligations to their babies, and the father naturally is in a good position to grant this. Be prepared for your wife to come up with many excuses why she can't take time off for herself. Don't allow your wife any room for excuses because she certainly will find them. Present her with definite plans for some time to herself: a gift certificate for an hour or two at a spa or a beauty parlor, an invitation for lunch at a friend's house, or a gift certificate for a shopping trip. To make sure she goes, you may want to drive her there.

One of the most common contributors to mother burnout is father walkout. An uninvolved or absentee husband and father eventually burns out the whole family. Jan, a committed mother of a high-need baby, came to me for consultation. One tip-off as to the cause of her burnout was the telltale statement, "My husband is spending longer and longer hours at the office." Their high-need baby required constant comforting and Dad felt inept as a baby comforter and a cry stopper. He delegated this entire job to Jan.

Not only was the baby not fun to be with, but Jan was not fun to be with either. As a result, Dad began withdrawing to the security and strokes of his profession and Jan became a burned-out mother and wife. After pointing out to Jan this cycle of escape fathering, I wrote her a prescription that said: "To Mrs. Burned-out, Apply one dose of a caring husband three times a day until symptoms subside; refill as needed." I asked Jan to prepare a candlelight dinner for her husband and put this prescription on his plate, then pour out her feelings and seek his help.

When you have the "burnout talk" with your wife, here are some practical topics to discuss. First, get her to admit that she is burning out. Next, point out to her that burnout is not good for the baby. Ask her to write down in order of importance all those factors that drain her energy from her baby and contribute to burnout. A patient of mine, Jack, following this talk with his wife, confided to me, "This wasn't so difficult after all. All that was needed is someone to come in and clean our house twice a week. That's a lot cheaper than a psychiatrist or a marriage counselor, and the results are quicker!"

22

~~~~~~

HELPING YOUR SON DEVELOP HEALTHY MASCULINITY

Sexuality researchers believe that fathers affect a child's attitude toward sexuality more than mothers do. Sexuality means more than just sex. It includes not only the physical characteristics and changes of the developing child, but also the feelings and attitudes associated with these physical qualities. There has been more research on fathers' effects on the development of sexual identity than on any other aspect of paternal influence. However, this discussion is based upon my own experience and opinions gleaned from 20 years in pediatric practice and counseling many families in ways to help their child to develop healthy sexual attitudes, as well as from the findings of reputable researchers whose views I value.

How a boy develops masculinity. "I don't want my son to grow up to be a pansy," exclaimed Mark, a new father. His sentiments are shared by most men. First, let me define what I mean by masculine. I do not mean aggressive, domineering, overbearing, punitive, bossy, loud, and violent. Instead, masculine means being assertive, decisive, responsible, logical, and able to take charge in difficult situations. These fundamental qualities should be founded on a basis of nurturing, tenderness, and ability to love and live. Masculine attitudes complement feminine attitudes. For better or for worse, I believe in "vive la difference." Although sex role differences

81

are not as clearly defined in today's families, I believe that differences between mothers and fathers are necessary for healthy sex role modeling. The healthiest sex role identification is found among children whose fathers clearly represent a healthy masculine role and whose mothers reflect a healthy feminine one.

The quality of fathering that a boy receives is the most critical factor in how he views himself as a male. A boy's masculinity correlates highly with the degree to which his father is available and how the father acts as a masculine member of the family. How your son perceives your masculinity is more important than how masculine you feel yourself to be. Studies have shown an important correlation between a child's perception of his father as a decision maker, limit setter, and disciplinarian and the development of strong masculine behavior in the son.

Become a nurturing father. One of the most important effects of fatherhood on a son's masculine development is when the son perceives the father as a *nurturing person.* Studies on this correlation have dispelled the myth that a nurturing father may create an effeminate boy. Our traditional view that *maternal* nurturing is the prime determinant of a child's emotional and social adjustment may be incomplete. The father's qualities play an equally if not more influential role. Paternal nurturing is *positively* related to a boy's and a girl's success in peer relationships, cognitive abilities, and successful vocational adjustments. If you appear very masculine, but do not demonstrate nurturing qualities, you may become a very weak role model for your son. In fact, some studies show a negative effect: A very masculine father who is not affectionate, encouraging, or nurturing may promote nonmasculine behavior in his son. Perhaps the son does not want to imitate his father's lack of nurturing behavior and withdraws from imitating any of his father's behaviors, especially his masculine traits. Machismo without tenderness makes for an ineffective sexual role model.

Be a participating house husband. By participating in what are felt to be traditional female activities (cooking, housework, and so on) you will not affect your son's masculinity. (Sorry dads, but research just doesn't support our lazy inclinations.) Doing housework is not hazardous to your child's sexual identity—or yours! The stereotype of the masculine, hardworking father whose only roles are breadwinner and child punisher, but who otherwise lies passively on a couch watching television, emotionally isolated from the rest of the family, is not a healthy model for children to witness.

Take charge of discipline. Studies also show that if a father consistently adopts a passive role in discipline and family decision making, the son is more likely to be less masculine. Be sensitive to how your child perceives husband-wife disagreements during decision making. A child should not feel that there is a winner or loser. A child should feel that you respect your wife's input and that major decisions are made together. This is especially important when the child wants a certain privilege and tries to play one parent against the other to obtain his goal.

I cannot stress enough the importance of a high level of father involvement at home as a major determinant in sexual role modeling. Fathers often have difficulty assuming the traditionally maternal tasks of child tending and housework. Mothers seem to sense that the child needs the total package: nurturing and limit setting. One without the other does not provide a healthy balance for an impressionable child. If a father does not provide structure and discipline in the home, the mother will. Although assertiveness in mothers and girls is as important a quality as tenderness is in fathers and boys, *balance* is necessary for healthy role modeling.

When Dad does not make this investment in the family, the mother must take up the slack and become both the mother and father, a confusing model for the child. When the father is available, both in mind and body, he can be more responsive to his son, thus reinforcing the child's approaches and encouraging him to reach out to his father more often. An involved and nurturing father provides more opportunities for his son to imitate his masculine behavior. The son of an absent or ineffective father is more likely to model his mother.

Match your interests to your son's abilities, not to your own. A mismatch of interests and abilities between the father and son increases the risk of the child developing an unhealthy sex role identification. For example, an intellectual father with a son who has few intellectual interests or a sports-minded father with a son who possesses little athletic ability are both high-risk situations. The son may feel that he is not valued because he does not measure up to his dad's interests and abilities. As a defense, the child may tune out this part of a father's personality and eventually may tune his dad out entirely. Let your child know that you value him for who he is, not how he performs. With our first two boys, I was guilty of imposing my interests and abilities on my sons.

Dads, I wish to repeat a very important principle of healthy sexual role modeling: *Be sure your child perceives that you value what and who he is, not how he performs.* Whether it be in academics, social endeavors, or sports, a child should not feel that his value is a measure of his performance. Each child should feel that his home is above this form of judgment. The healthiest sexual attitudes develop in children who have two involved and committed parents modeling healthy masculine and feminine roles.

23

HOW TO HELP YOUR DAUGHTER DEVELOP HEALTHY FEMININITY

Research suggests that fathers may play an even more important role than mothers in a daughter's development of healthy sexual identity. Fathers are powerful reinforcers of their children's behavior. A child learns to repeat those behaviors that parents reward and to shy away from behaviors that go unrewarded. Fathers, consciously or unconsciously, reinforce sexual development in their daughters. A father may without thinking, for example, encourage his daughters to participate in less aggressive, less competitive activities like drama, ballet, music, or cheerleading rather than encourage her to take an active part in sports. I confess to channeling my daughters into stereotyped feminine roles. I love ballet, and even before becoming a father I told my wife that if we had a daughter I wanted her to be a ballerina. Because of my encouragement, our eight-year-old daughter, Hayden, enrolled in ballet classes. After a few months, Hayden decided to give up ballet and play softball!

Although you may not always consciously realize that you are reinforcing your daughter's feminine personality traits, what is important is how your daughter thinks that you perceive her. Fathers tend to engage in more rough-and-tumble physical play with sons and more cuddling, softer types of activities with daughters. The gentler way that you play with your daughter tells her that you regard her as sensitive and delicate and that she had better be delicate. As I will discuss later, I believe it is healthy to engage in a bit of sexual stereotyping as long as Dad exercises wisdom and balance in steering his son or daughter in activities more becoming to one or the other sex (although which activities go with which sex is becoming more and more blurred). Personally, I abhor the trend toward unisexism because I feel it devalues the uniqueness of each sex.

Father as nurturer. As I stressed earlier in discussing the importance of a nurturing father on a son's masculinity, a nurturing father also greatly influences the development of his daughter's femininity. Studies show that girls who are raised in a home where the mother dominates and the father is passive, uninvolved in decision making and nonnurturing, are more likely to have difficulty being comfortable with males later on. *Girls and women do not regard tenderness and nurturing as a weakness or a nonmasculine trait in a man.* This is a male misconception that I wish to strongly downplay. Fathers tend to treat sons and daughters differently and this differential treatment may positively or negatively affect a child's sexual identity. Fathers tend to punish girls and boys differently, using more corporal punishment on boys. Could this be a way of reinforcing aggression in boys while encouraging delicacy in girls? Fathers are often more tolerant of academic underachievement in girls than in boys. Another true confession: Upon receiving the news from school that one of our daughters may have a reading disability, my first thought was, "That shouldn't bother her too much because she is more into arts and may not pursue a highly academic career anyway." However, I would have been immediately concerned if this learning disability appeared in one of our boys! I soon realized that our daughter's future

86

career plans may require a college degree, so we got her the extra help she needed.

The sex of the child you wanted is not what you got. Some fathers may have wanted a son instead of a daughter. They may never have "forgiven" the girl for not being a boy and may reinforce "boy" activities, showing satisfaction with tomboy behavior and discontent with more traditionally feminine pursuits. My wife, Martha, recalls how much her father wanted boys, but instead had two girls. She spent the first three years of her life being called "Butch."

Fathers also tend to accept a boy with a difficult temperament more than a girl with the same trait. Disruptive behavior from a son may be excused with "Oh, he's just being a boy!" whereas the same behavior in a girl is not acceptable. It is healthy for fathers to have a wider acceptance of children with more difficult temperaments, i.e. high-need children. Temperament differences should have no sexual discrimination.

Watch how you treat your wife. Children are very perceptive about how their parents treat one another. In your role as parents, you are always on stage before your children. How the father treats the mother especially affects the daughter's femininity. If a man is involved, loving, supportive, and rewarding of his wife's mothering, the daughter not only has a healthier definition of maleness and fatherhood, but she also has a higher regard for the value of her own femininity.

All in all, the healthiest home environment is one in which the father behaves as a strong, nurturing, and masculine person toward his child and toward the mother, and a mother behaves as a naturally feminine person toward both the father and child. It is this goal that I wish fathers to strive for in their homes.

24

SINGLE FATHERING

Separation from the spouse by death or by divorce may leave a dad in the unusual role of single fathering. The following are some tips on making the best of a less-than-ideal situation—for yourself and your child.

When divorce seems imminent, tell your child exactly what your role will be in your child's care. Children are bound to feel that not only is "Mommy losing Daddy" but they are "losing Daddy also." It is important for Father to impress upon his children that they have not lost a father. The child needs to understand how the father-child relationship will continue (e.g., where Daddy will live, how often you will see her). Defining the father's role exactly may, of course, be difficult, because many fathers may not have answered these questions yet in their own minds.

Tell your child how often you plan to visit. The younger the child, the more frequent your visits should be. Younger children cannot really conceptualize time, so the statement "once a week" may not mean much to the child under age five. Ideally, visiting a young child should be similar to his feeding schedule—small, frequent visits on an as-needed basis. Fortunately, rigid visiting schedules are not as common as they used to be, especially with the trend toward dual custody.

Older children should be consulted in working out a visiting arrangement that respects the busy schedule of a school-aged child. Scheduled visiting rights are somewhat artificial, especially for older children. The children may have some important activity and may be ambivalent about spending a weekend with Dad. Perhaps an open visiting arrangement is more realistic for older children. For example, Dad could call up and say, "How would you like to go to dinner or go to a ball game tonight?" This gives the child the option.

Avoid the "Disneyland Daddy" syndrome. Spending every weekend with Dad is a situation far removed from the reality of family life and can be confusing to the child. These weekends also may be unrealistic because they often consist entirely of fun and games, which is totally different from a child's "other life" at home. Occasional "Disneyland time" is fun for a child, but a steady diet is not a realistic way of life. To regard time with Dad as all "fun" and time with Mom as "all discipline" is not a balanced diet, and the child becomes confused as to which is "real life."

Be consistent in discipline. It is necessary for the custodial parent, usually the mother, to run a tight ship. It is unfair to the child and to the parents for Dad to have no discipline with the child during his visits. As a result, Mom becomes the "bad guy" and the father becomes the "fun person." Sometimes the child becomes confused and/or worse learns to play one parent against the other.

Following their parents' divorce or the death of one parent, it is common for children to become more difficult to discipline. It is a time when a parent relaxes the discipline the most—because you also are trying to get your own life organized. It is common for older children to try to figure out which parent is the "bad guy" in the divorce. He may become an ally of one parent and become angry at the other. The older child also may be more sensitive to the loneliness of his parents and may try to assume the role of a friend or companion or even partner or substitute to an unhappy parent. These are not unhealthy roles as long as the compassionate child does not keep too much inside himself while attempting to comfort the parent. Expect behavioral changes following death or divorce. Your child may crave attention and not let you out of his sight. Your child may also feel he is to blame for the divorce. The increased energy demands will put an added strain on you at the very time you are struggling to get your own life back on track.

Adolescence may be the most difficult to deal with. Adolescents often become very judgmental about who is at fault. Following a divorce, adolescents are very prone to jump into instant love affairs and sexual gratifications. Adolescents are particularly judgmental about the sexual activities of their parents. Be discreet about your sexual pursuits in front of your children and do not expect your children to instantly warm up to a "girlfriend."

Listen to your child. Encourage your child to ventilate his or her feelings about life with you and life with the mother. The more your child can freely talk to you about his own adjustment to life after divorce (or death of the mother) the better able he will be to adjust to this new lifestyle—and so will you.

Be approachable. Give your children a message, "Even though Dad will not be living in the house, I always will be your father." Be sure they know where you live, where you work, your phone number, and how to reach you. Encourage your child to call you frequently and be sure you are approachable when he does. If your child constantly gets a "busy signal," this may reinforce the suspicion that already is building up—Dad no longer is interested in living at home and no longer is interested in me."

Teachable moments. There is a tendency for the non-custodial parent, usually the father, to structure the time with the child and want to "do something fun and meaningful" every minute of the day. Children are not like this; neither is real life. Children are very *mood dependent.* They may be in a mood for sports and a vigorous activity or they may be in the mood to sit quietly and do nothing. A valuable concept I have learned from our children is that of "teachable moments." Simply spend a lot of unstructured time with your child and allow circumstances to open the door to a meaningful interaction.

You may be walking in the woods some day and stumble on an interesting scene. This may trigger an idea in your mind, such as sitting down on a log and telling your child a story "that reminds me of the time I was a boy . . ." Spontaneous thoughts and activities that arise during time with your child are often more meaningful and lasting. Give your child memories. There may be a lot of bad memories, especially surrounding a divorce. Spending time with your child doing memorable things, playing ball, going to the movies, hiking, camping, are all filed away in the child's mind later to be recalled as special times with Dad. Whatever your custodial role is as a single father, it is vital that your child always carry in his memory that he has a dad—and a very involved one.

25

wwwwwwwwwwwwwwwwwwwwwwwwwwwwwwwwwwwwwwwwwwwwwwwwwww

PLAY TIPS FOR FATHERS—BIRTH TO THREE MONTHS

M ost fathers truly enjoy being with their baby, but they often confide in me, "I've run out of things to do with him! In a couple of years when he is old enough to throw a ball it will be easy for me, but how do you play with a baby?" The following are a few tips to help the father and baby enjoy each other more.

Give your baby lots of eye-to-eye contact and face-to-face contact. Because of your newborn's limited visual ability, you may feel that you're not really connected to your baby when you try to maintain eye contact. A newborn's vision develops slowly, as if the lens on the camera is being brought into focus. In the first two weeks, your baby can see you, but your image may be a bit blurry.

Around two weeks of age, you may notice that your baby begins to stare at you longer. At this age, babies see most clearly if your face is within 12 to 18 inches. To determine the distance at which your baby can see your face most clearly, move her toward and away from you at a distance between 1 and 2 feet. The point at which your baby stares most intently at your face is the distance at which you are most in focus. You may notice that your baby's eyes fix on your eyes for a fleeting second or two when she scans your face.

In the early months, babies become easily bored and quickly lose interest in figures that don't move. This is one reason that the human face is attractive to babies because it constantly changes to hold their interests. Babies hold their visual attention span longer to images that have a lot of light and dark contrast, like the human face. Here is where the father may have a bit of an edge; his generally more contrasting features often will hold baby's attention longer. Practice the game of engaging your baby in face-to-face contact between the distance of 12 and 18 inches. Be animated, constantly changing your facial gestures. You will find that after several weeks of practicing this game, you will increase the holding power of your baby's attention.

At about two months of age, you will notice that your baby's visual attention span greatly improves. Your baby will tend to stare at you longer, as if studying your face. It is a beautiful feeling when your baby looks into your eyes as if to say, "Hi, Dad, I enjoy looking at your face." When you notice your baby holding a fix on your face for more than just a few seconds, this is the time you could begin playing imitation games.

Facial gestures are fascinating to a baby. Stick your tongue out, open your eyes wide, open your mouth wide, and develop fun facial contortions. At about three to four months, babies may even imitate your facial gestures. Visual games help your baby get to know your face. They also develop your ability to hold the attention of your baby. Developing this holding power with your baby will enable her to enjoy longer play periods with you without losing interest.

I've always valued the attention holding power of the human face and wanted my babies to get hooked on my face also, because a baby usually spends most of his or her day looking into the mother's face.

Talk and sing to your baby. Don't be disappointed if your baby seems to show a preference for the mother's voice. Tiny babies prefer higher-pitched female voices, particularly their own mother's. But, dads, take heart. Your voice has some unique fascinations for your baby. Women talk differently to babies than men. Mothers develop a unique baby talk by exhibiting a lot of inflections in her voice, constant crescendo, decrescendo, and exaggerating vowels, such as "gooood baaaaaby!" Fathers, however, talk in relatively monotonous tones of voice, in a lower pitch, droning and with less inflection. In some ways then, a father's voice is often more calming to a baby than a mother's.

Each day during my son Stephen's first year, he and I would have our special walking and singing time. I would nestle him in my arms with his head under my chin, or as he got older, placed him on my shoulder, and we would take a 10- to 15-minute walk while I sang to him. You will notice that your baby prefers certain tunes. Remember which ones your baby prefers and repeat them as often as you can. Often the baby prefers your homemade songs. Our sixth child, Matthew, enjoyed the "Daddy loves Matthew" song that I made up, and I'm no songwriter!

Tub time together. Another way you can have fun with your baby is to take him into the bathtub for a nice warm, skin-to-skin soak together. Your baby can lie on your chest, half in and half out of the water. Keep the water at an even temperature with a slow trickle of warm water from the faucet. You also can stroke your baby and slosh water gently over his limbs and torso. Besides cleaning the baby and frequently freeing Mom from this ritual, your baby will learn to enjoy water. A before bedtime bath is often a good way to soothe a fussy baby, especially when Mom is frazzled and not able to comfort the baby.

Toys at this stage. During the first few months, parents are the primary playmates, however, appropriate toys are a welcome addition as the baby's interests widen. When you select a toy for your baby, look at them from your baby's point of view and take into account your baby's capabilities and preferences at each stage and development. An important principle in choosing a toy at this stage, and all others, is contingency play—the action of the toy is contingent upon the action of the baby.

For example, kicking or batting at a dangling object or shaking a rattle will produce both movement and sound. Your baby will learn that she has an effect on her surroundings and, therefore, will develop competence. Black-and-white toys hold a baby's attention longer. Black-and-white mobiles, black-and-white balls, or a paper plate with black-and-white dots or lines are favorites at this stage. Sit your baby in an infant seat and dangle a black-and-white mobile within striking range—approximately 6 to 12 inches from his torso or from his feet. The baby will enjoy batting at, hitting, and kicking the dangling mobile. (A play tip: The baby's play attention span is longer if she sits up in an infant seat at a 30 to 45 degree angle rather than lying on her back.)

Massage your baby. In the early months, babies often are tense and tight. Massage can help relax and loosen up the tense baby. There is much focus on a baby getting used to the mother's body, but it is also important that your baby get used to a masculine touch.

Playing with your baby is not only good for his or her development, but it helps you become more acquainted and comfortable handling your baby. When you see how much your baby enjoys being with you, the more comfortable you will be playing with your baby and the more you will enjoy the experience.

26

~~~~~~

PLAYING WITH YOUR BABY—THREE TO SIX MONTHS

Most fathers find it is easier to play with their babies at the beginning of three months of age, because babies can do more. You will notice that your baby's activity becomes more purposeful as if he is putting more thought into what he does. In the first three months, babies' muscles are rather tight and their hands and feet are drawn inward toward themselves. At around three months, babies enjoy playing with their hands. This is the reach out and touch someone stage. Baby will love playing with your beard, mustache, hair, and glasses and exploring your face, nose, and ears.

A baby can do a lot of things with a bracelet or bracelet-like ring. He can grab it with one hand, bring it toward his body, or grab it with the other hand, pull on it with both hands, release with one hand while holding on with the other, follow it with his eyes, and gum the bracelet as it inevitably finds its way to its final destination—his mouth. I have enjoyed many sessions playing tug of war with Matthew. We call this, "Grab the bracelet from Daddy." As the baby grows and becomes more tenacious, you will have increasing difficulty getting the bracelet back.

Open-eyes, open-hand signs. Watch for signs that your baby is eager to play with you. When the baby is very alert, excited, or interested, his hands are wide open with one or both arms up. You will get the feeling he is giving you a "come on" with his hands. This is his invitation to play. As previously mentioned, a wise principle of play and learning for the baby is that baby-initiated play has more learning value and can be sustained for a longer period of time than activity initiated by you.

Keep in mind, babies are very mood dependent when it comes to play. Your baby may be in the mood for quiet nesting rather than a stimulating physical activity. Take cues from your baby and try to adjust your playful interaction according to your baby's moods. "Rolling-type" play is fun at this age. At about five months, babies love to climb and roll over foam cushions, wedges, and cylinders.

Prior to six months, babies do not have the motor skills to entertain themselves for very long periods of time. During the first six months of age, parents are their main entertainers.

Block play. At five to six months of age, babies develop reaching and grasping skills and are able to play with the most time-tested favorite of all toys, blocks. If babies quickly become bored with any single type of play activity at this stage, try the following activity to increase your baby's attention span in playing with blocks. Place your baby in a high chair next to a table and put three 1-inch square blocks within reaching distance on a towel or tablecloth. You may use black-and-white or contrasting color blocks. Station yourself and your wife or a sibling at each end of the table. Pull back and forth on the tablecloth or towel, slowly moving the blocks in front of the baby. He will be fascinated by these moving objects and will amaze you with the high percentage of direct hits as his chubby little hands pounce quickly on the moving blocks.

27

PLAYING WITH YOUR
BABY—SIX TO NINE
MONTHS

At about six months of age, babies can begin entertaining themselves for longer periods of time because a very important developmental skill clicks in—the ability to sit up without support. You can now put your baby down on the floor and she can sit for varying periods of time (usually 5 to 15 minutes), engaging in attentive play.

Father's play circle. Between six and eight months, set your baby in front of you along with a few favorite toys and make a circle around her with your legs. Within this intimate space, father and baby can enjoy hand-to-hand play as they sit on the floor in this circle.

Climb on Pop. From six to nine months, babies begin to crawl and climb. Lie down on the floor and set your baby next to you. Dangle an enticing toy on the other side of your body, encouraging the baby to climb over you to get the toy. Your baby soon will realize that climbing on Pop is fun. As a variant of climbing on Pop, at around eight to nine months, babies learn to stop halfway through their climb and sit on Dad's tummy. You may want to add more fun by bouncing your baby!

Crawling on Dad. Another major developmental skill that clicks in during this stage is crawling, a skill that brings about more fun activities to do with Dad. Here's how you can learn about your baby's crawling. A baby's crawling style is as individual as her personality. Babies' first attempts at locomotion are a series of arm, leg, and torso movements coordinated as babies learn that they have "wheels" and learn how to "roll" on them. The arms and legs kick and push with swimming movements that are directed outward from the body, not downward toward the floor. At first, babies are unable to get their tummies off the ground. They may worm their way across the floor in a type of commando crawl, using only their backs and arms, pivoting the upper trunk and circular movements, while dragging their hips and legs on the floor. Some babies use their legs for propulsion and their arms to steer.

When refining the art of crawling, the baby gradually gets more and more of her body off the ground. At first, the tummy is elevated off the ground and the baby rocks back and forth on her knees and elbows. With time and practice, the baby learns to crawl forward and backward, a type of crab crawl, on her hands and knees. The baby gradually finds her ground transportation by developing the skill of cross-crawling—the arm on the right side coordinates with the leg on the left and vice versa.

Here's a fun activity for Dad—cross-crawl with your baby. Get down on the floor next to your baby and crawl with her. You will notice that this style of crawling is the most efficient, speedy, and balanced. Watching the father and baby cross-crawling across the room is bound to cause a reaction from onlookers. Developing locomotor skills not only enables a baby to get from one place to another, it is also an exercise in problem solving, another sign of emerging intelligence. If the baby wants a toy that is a few feet away, she must learn to use her body parts in an efficient way that will enable her to reach the toy. Play the "come-get-the-toy game." Place an enticing toy increasingly longer distances away from your baby, encouraging her to crawl toward the toy.

At around seven months, a baby no longer is content to be in your arms and lap. She usually wants to be put down so that she can get closer to whatever is interesting on the floor. She will want Dad to get down on the floor with her.

Newspaper play. Mothers often complain about their husbands spending too much time with their faces buried in the newspaper. Babies love to sit on Daddy's lap and "read" the newspaper, too! Remember, babies are very interested in looking at things with sharp black-and-white contrast. Newspaper print fits this description. Don't plan to get much reading done beyond the headlines, because your baby usually will bat at, grab, and want to crumble the paper. Wives usually don't complain about husbands spending too much time buried beneath the newspaper when Daddy and the baby do this together.

28

PLAYING WITH YOUR BABY—NINE TO TWELVE MONTHS

This is one of the favorite play stages for fathers because the baby can move and do more. At around nine months of age, most babies begin to separate from their mother and show an increased interest in their father, which stimulates fathers to be more interested in their babies. But, dads, don't feel left out if your baby still prefers his mother as a source of comfort. This is normal.

The main developmental accomplishment at this stage is going from crawling to walking. This skill brings about a change in play activities. Babies love to crawl over to Dad and scale your pant legs. When you walk into the room, your baby will crawl over to you, grab a hold of your leg, and pull himself to a standing position by using your trousers for support. At this stage, babies begin to initiate play. If you have been responsive to your baby's cues during the first nine months, your baby will trust you and will begin to approach you. When I come home from work, Martha says to Stephen, "Daddy's coming home!" He responds by crawling to the front door and greeting me with the familiar pant leg pull as if to say, "Now let's play."

Walking with Dad. Babies love to hold on to Dad for support when beginning to walk. Begin with the two-handed assist, holding your baby's hands in front of you with both of yours. When your baby masters this skill, progress to the one-handed assist, with your baby walking alongside you. Walking with Dad is not only a new and fun activity, it also contributes to the development of trust between the father and infant. It is the beginning of a long relationship in which the child learns to lean on Dad.

Play the hide-the-toy game with your baby. Between nine and twelve months of age, babies begin to remember where things are, to show a longer attention span, and are able to make decisions during toy play. In the earlier stages of your baby's development, out of sight is out of mind. If you hide a toy in your hand, the baby acts as if the toy no longer exists and shows no interest in playing with it. Between nine and twelve months, babies develop the mental skill of object permanence, meaning they can remember what they have seen even though it is out of sight. Here's how to play the game of "hide-the-toy" with your baby. Let your baby watch you hide a favorite toy in your hand and then put both hands behind your back. Bring your hands out in front again with the same hand containing the toy.

These games may not appear very interesting to some "big men," but they are a way of helping you get to know your baby. Playing simple games with your baby and gradually increasing their complexity helps you know where your baby's development is and what he is capable of doing. While your baby is growing and developing skills, you are developing your powers of observation and your ability to understand your baby. This sets the stage for one of the father's major roles within the next year, discipline. In order to effectively discipline your child, you must begin with a realistic understanding of his capabilities at each stage of development. Playing with your baby improves your skills as a baby watcher.

Play ball! Finally the long awaited father-baby ball game is a favorite at this stage. Babies love to pitch a ball and fetch it. Use a small, hand-size, lightweight plastic ball, like a table tennis ball. It makes an interesting noise bouncing on a hard floor and moves quickly. Talk to your baby about the game such as, "Get the ball and throw it to Dad." Give one direction first, "get the ball"—and then after your baby has retrieved the ball, add "throw the ball to Daddy." Babies at this stage cannot comprehend two instructions at once. You have to break them up.

Gesture games are favorites at this stage. Babies love to imitate and respond to fun words accompanied by gestures, such as "pat-a-cake" and "peekaboo." Although babies cannot say much at this stage, they can mimic your gestures letting you know that they really are tuned in to the game. For example, after playing many games of pat-a-cake with your baby, try saying, "pat-a-cake" without moving your hands. The baby often will take your verbal cues and begin to clap his hands, as if you touched off a pattern that has been stored in his memory. Be sure, then, to reinforce his gestures by joining in the game. Keep the game going as long as you can because babies lose interest very quickly. Don't feel like your baby is losing interest in you when he loses interest in the game. The average one-year-old seems to have an attention span of less than one minute and then wants to move on to something else.

Dads, it is normal to sometimes feel that you are "just wasting time" when you play games like stacking blocks or pat-a-cake. You may feel that you should be "doing something important" instead. What may seem like meaningless activity to you means a lot to your baby. The more interest you show in your baby early on, the more interest your child will show in you. Play stacks up to be a good long-term investment!

29

THE FATHER'S ROLE IN DISCIPLINE—BIRTH TO ONE YEAR

D iscipline begins in the early months. One day I was giving a seminar to a group of new fathers. The subject was how to discipline. In the first part of the seminar I spoke about the importance of fathers bonding with their babies at birth, carrying their babies a lot, being involved in their everyday care, and all the nurturing aspects of good fathering. Partway through the seminar a father impatiently asked, "Can we start talking about discipline now? When do I spank my child?" This father released the feelings that many men have—discipline is punishment. How wrong that concept is. Punishment is only one aspect of discipline, and a small one at that. I went on to explain to the fathers in the seminar that everything we had been talking about was part of discipline!

Discipline is basically an attitude within a child and an atmosphere in your home that makes punishment less necessary. When punishment is necessary, it is more appropriately administered. The foundations of discipline are laid in the early months of a baby's life by two important relationships: *Getting to know your child* and *helping your child feel right.* A child who feels right is more likely to act right and is easier to discipline. By spending a lot of time with your baby in the early months, you get to know your baby—how your baby acts and his preferences and capabilities; you get a feeling of the personality of your baby and knowledge of your baby's normal behavior. By understanding your baby's normal behavior early on, you begin to have more of an appreciation of what becomes abnormal behavior when the baby becomes a toddler. By spending a lot of time with a baby during the first year, you begin to have realistic expectations of what normal infant behavior is all about. Normally, babies do pull on light cords, drop things a lot, get into things, and spread a lot of objects around the house. By spending a lot of time with your baby, you become a keener baby watcher. By knowing your baby, you become a more effective disciplinarian later on.

Become a baby nurturer first. In order for a father to become an effective disciplinarian, he must first become a baby nurturer. Years ago, a group of researchers interviewed teenagers asking them what qualities made their father an effective disciplinarian. The teenagers remembered that their fathers were fair limit setters and sensitive nurturers. The latter quality is why discipline begins early in infancy. By carrying your baby a lot, responding to your baby's cry, becoming a sensitive baby comforter, and simply spending a lot of time with your baby you will become a nurturing father.

The more you nurture your baby, the more your baby trusts you. *Trust is the basis of discipline.* In asking fathers what they most want in being a disciplinarian they often answer, "I want to be the authority figure in our home." Authority is based upon trust. In order for your child to regard you as an authority figure, she must first trust you. This is where becoming a nurturing father early in infancy really pays off. When a baby trusts you, your baby develops an inner feeling of rightness that forms the basis of the baby's behavior.

A baby who feels right on the inside is more likely to act right on the outside. A child's outward behavior mirrors her inward feelings. When your baby trusts you, she is more likely to regard you as an authority figure. Imagine, if you can, how you regard your own authority figures. Those whom you respect and trust the most are those you are more likely to look up to as an authority figure. Establishing a feeling of trust between a father and an infant during the first year is the beginning of discipline. A simple father-infant interaction, for example, is when the baby cries, the father promptly responds to the cry and picks up and comforts the baby. This may be your first "disciplinary action." A baby learns that she is in a home where the father is responsive to her needs. This is how authority begins. One day in my office I was watching a father interact with his infant. He held the baby a lot and engaged in frequent eye-to-eye contact, and he gave a nurtured response to the baby's cry. I couldn't help admiring this father's nurturing abilities and said, "David, you're a good disciplinarian." Surprised, he replied, "But I don't spank my baby!" I went on to explain how nurturing was building up trust between the father and baby.

What about the father who takes the heavy-handed approach to discipline and becomes a firm disciplinarian around the second year? He was not involved much during the first year because he felt that was primarily the mother's job and decided he would take over the disciplining as soon as a conflict of wills began. This father may not be an effective disciplinarian for several reasons. First, the father and baby have not built up a trusting relationship and the baby operates from a basis of mistrust. The baby may operate from an inner feeling of anxiety rather than rightness. A baby who does not feel right inside is more likely not to act right on the outside.

The father who has not given a nurturing response to the baby's needs during the first year and was more restraining in his nurturing runs the risk of having a baby who operates from the basis of anger.

Angry children are the most difficult to discipline. The baby does not have a trusting relationship with the father and therefore does not regard the father as a trusted authority figure. Because a father has not spent a lot of time with the baby during the first year, he also has not learned to read his baby's behavior during the first year so he will not be an astute baby watcher during the second year. He does not have realistic expectations of toddler behavior because he did not invest the time early on.

The father who has not invested his time in the first year becoming a nurturing father is more likely to regard discipline as corporal punishment and unwisely will fall into the spanking trap. The father honestly believes he is doing the right thing because he equates discipline with punishment. He begins trying to control the infant's behavior by spanking. Unfortunately, it seldom works and, worst of all, spanking causes a distance to develop between the parent and child. This scenario seldom leads to a good discipline relationship.

Becoming a nurturing father during the first year of life lays a good foundation for discipline during the next stages of the infant's development—it teaches the infant to respect his father as a trusted authority figure.

30

THE FATHER'S ROLE IN DISCIPLINE—THE TODDLER

Most toddlers are impulsive. It is this impulsiveness that gets them into trouble. This is why I emphasize the importance of the nurturing relationship during the first two years. Spending a lot of time holding and comforting your baby mellows impulsive temperament, resulting in impulsive babies behaving in a more organized manner. An organized child is easier to discipline. Impulsive toddlers need limit setting and this becomes the primary role of the father from the second year on. Limit setting without nurturing usually fails. A father comes across only as a "no" person, heavy-handed, stern, punitive, and authoritarian. He is likely to be an ineffective disciplinarian. Sometimes fathers are hesitant to become too affectionate and nurturing for fear that the child will become manipulative and will never learn to obey. Actually, the opposite is true. Being affectionate allows fathers to be more firm about setting limits.

The world of most toddlers is somewhat chaotic and disorganized. The father provides structure and discipline. A child wants and needs limits set by a trusted person in authority. Picture what is going on in this young bundle of energy, driven in all directions by whim and impulse. If a child's energy is not harnessed, he will waste it by going in many frivolous directions, often exerting a lot of effort, but achieving little. If, however, there is structure in the child's life, he feels more secure because someone has channeled his energies into a meaningful direction. Being a director of a child's energy is another important disciplinary role for the father. A father's role in discipline during the first year was primarily that of nurturer. During the second year, the toddler stage, the father's role widens into that of an authority figure and a designer of a child's safe environment.

Discipline begins by having realistic expectations of toddler behavior. Fathers often are confused about what toddlers are like. They often confuse normal toddler curiosity with misbehavior. Fathers' unrealistic expectations of toddler behavior often lead to mother-father conflicts. Mothers usually are more accepting of a wide range of toddler behavior, whereas fathers tend to place more restrictions on young children. This is not always bad. A more restrictive father helps to balance an overly tolerant mother.

Toddlers are driven by intense curiosity that overrules consideration and safety. One of the father's roles as a disciplinarian is to protect the toddler from his own impulses. Toddlers are naturally impulsive. This is how they learn. Expect your toddler, who loves to climb, to frequently crawl up on your desk and "rearrange" your papers. We call this "clearing the deck." Expect your toddler to have a fascination with turning the television knobs. These constant hassles are normal toddler behavior. You may find yourself saying "no" a thousand times.

Alternatives to "no." Between twelve and fifteen months of age, most babies can understand that "no" means stop what they are doing, but they seldom understand the reason they should not tug on the lamp cord or pull off the television knobs. If your baby has grown accustomed to your usual tone of voice during play, she will be uniquely sensitive to your language of displeasure. You don't have to yell "no" in an angry, harsh, and upsetting tone of voice. If, during the first year, you have developed this mutual sensitivity, a firm "no, stop, don't touch" accompanied by picking the baby up, looking him squarely in the eye, and removing her from the scene usually will get the point across. Dads, keep in mind that some babies take longer to get the point than others. You may have to say "no" and remove her ten times before it actually sinks in. Personally, I often find it easier simply to move the temptations to a higher place until the child is older.

One of the difficulties that fathers often share with me is their confusion over how much their baby really understands. A good rule of thumb is to imagine how much of your discipline you think gets through to your toddler and then double it. Toddlers understand far more than we think they do. When it comes to protecting your curious toddler from her environment and your home furnishings from her curiosity, strive to balance the right amount of freedom to explore her environment with the restraints necessary to prevent her from hurting herself or your furnishings. Toddlers need and expect this protection from both their mother and father.

How fathers may handle temper tantrums. During the second year, expect your toddler to throw frequent temper tantrums. A temper tantrum results in the need the toddler has to explore her environment. In order to learn and develop their mental and motor skills, toddlers need to explore and get their hands on everything in their environment, but the intense desire to explore also exceeds the toddler's capabilities. This leads to frustration. Being able to get around by herself makes a toddler feel big and grown-up. This propels her to test the limits of her environment: to pull on tablecloths, turn knobs, climb up on tables, and so on.

Do not expect your toddler to first think of right and wrong or the safety of her actions. She simply is driven to act. When someone descends on her suddenly, someone she loves and trusts, with a loud "no," a conflict of wills results. Do not expect your strong willed toddler to respect a second opinion from you. When you remove her from the top of the table, expect an occasional angry tantrum. Your toddler does not yet have the ability to express her anger in language; she does so through an action—a tantrum. The outward show of emotion, such as anger and frustration, is a newly found ability that your toddler should be free to express and learn from. Here's how you can help your child during a tantrum.

A child is out of control during a tantrum and needs a trusted parent to help him regain his control. As he is screaming and flailing his arms and his behavior disintegrates right in front of you, realize that he is probably saying, "Help me, I'm out of control. Protect me from myself." Realizing that you cannot stop a tantrum nor can you handle it, the best you can do is support your child during the tantrum. Help him regain control. Be available for support when your emotionally drained child needs refueling. Sometimes when one of our children has gotten out of control, I pick him up and hold him firmly and lovingly in my arms while talking to him in a sensitive and caring voice, "Matthew, you're upset and Daddy wants to help. I'm going to hold you until you stop crying, because I love you." Expect your child to initially kick in protest for taking charge, but after he realizes that you are in control, he finally will melt exhausted in your arms. This will reinforce your child's feelings of trust in you. Taking charge of a two-year-old's tantrum is similar to comforting the fussy baby during the first year. You show your child that you are powerful, but nonthreatening, by giving your child the message that you care and therefore you are going to take charge. This is the same message that you gave your infant during the first year, "Distress is followed by comfort. I am a comforting father." As I mentioned earlier, comforting your toddler during a tantrum builds trust, trust is the basis of authority, and a trusted authority figure becomes an effective disciplinarian.

I don't wish to minimize the difficulty in handling a temper tantrum. *Staying calm is especially difficult for fathers because tantrums pose a threat to their authority and power.* You may feel, "How can this tiny child turn me into an emotional wreck?" Being unable to stop a child's tantrum can lead to outbursts of anger from the father, resulting in a shouting match between the father and child, and no one wins. I have seen occasions when a child throws a tantrum, the father responds by starting a shouting match, and pretty soon both are out of control and the mother has to take charge of both "children." This scene is not healthy role modeling for the observant child. Fortunately, temper tantrums usually subside between two to three years of age when the child becomes more verbal and is able to express his feelings with words rather than actions.

31

~~~~~~

THE FATHER'S ROLE IN DISCIPLINE—THE OLDER CHILD

I f you have laid the foundation of a nurturing father during the first two years, disciplining the older child, mainly in setting limits, is made much easier. Fathers may ask, "But what if I have not been an involved father during the first two years and really have not been a nurturing father, can I still become a good disciplinarian?" Yes. Fortunately, children are very resilient. The earlier you become involved, the easier it is to discipline. Some fathers suddenly emerge into the family scene around two years of age and want to suddenly become the main disciplinarian. Instant intimacy seldom happens. Take time to develop a relationship with your child. If you are starting from scratch, first become a nurturing father to your child and then weave in that role as you set limits. I cannot overemphasize that limit setting *plus nurturing* is necessary to become an effective disciplinarian. Without the foundation of nurturing, the trust necessary for your child to respond to your new role as limit setter may fail.

Be sure your child has a clear understanding of what behavior is expected of him. This is necessary for you to become a fair limit setter. Let me share with you an example of limit setting that occurred in our family. Our three-year-old, Erin, had a desire to ride her tricycle out into the street. I first told Erin where she may ride her tricycle, where she may not, and what the consequences would be if she disobeyed. I repeated them to her several times to be sure that she understood the directions and asked her, "Erin, do you understand why you are not to ride your tricycle out into the street?" I had her repeat the directions several times. Older children usually are not willfully defiant, but rather show childish irresponsibility by "forgetting." The instructions might go something like this, "Erin, because Daddy loves you very much, you must ride your tricycle only in these places (notice that I use a positive direction—where she should ride, and not a negative direction—where she should not). "Because we love you, I want you to promise me that you will only ride your tricycle in these places. Do you understand, Erin?" Meanwhile, you are holding your child and looking at her squarely in the eye with a firm voice of authority and a caring look of affection. Wait for her response and be sure that she clearly repeats your directions.

A father's disciplining role is to create the framework around which a child can operate. In this situation, Erin has been given the framework in which to operate, and she understands. As a trusted authority figure, you may then add, "I don't expect to see you riding your tricycle in the street. That would make Dad very unhappy and I would put the tricycle in the garage for a long time and you couldn't ride it." It is important that your child understands the nature of what you expect of him or her and the consequences of disobedience.

Some fathers feel that it is the nature of a child to obey. A child must obey simply because he is a child and you are his father. Although you may wish that this is true, in reality it isn't. Real obedience is motivated by respect. Respect is based on trust and the foundation of trust is laid during the first year of life. Obedience without respect does not lead to healthy discipline. You can beat a child into obedience, but you cannot force a child to respect his father. Respect for authority is the most important factor in effective discipline. Respecting means to honor someone. By becoming a nurturing father during the early years of life, the child learns to honor and respect his parents. Fathers may not think they are disciplining when they pick up a crying baby, but they are. The tiny baby whose distress signals are listened to learns that his care givers are in charge of helping and organizing him. A child must know who is in charge.

The parents who show that they are in charge of a crying baby by tending to his needs are more likely to be the ones who take charge of a distressed child as well. Caring for your baby during the first year of life truly prepares the father for the many disciplinarian encounters in later years. Learning how to sensitively console the colicky baby prepares you for taking charge of a toddler during a temper tantrum. Dads, get hooked on your babies! Carrying your baby, consoling your baby, playing with your baby, loving your baby *in the early years*—that's discipline!

Use an analogy of a game. A helpful way to explain rules to an older child is to make them seem like a familiar game. You may say: "Erin, anytime a group of people live and play together, then they must have rules. Otherwise people get hurt and nobody has any fun. It's like your soccer game. You have to play by the rules or you get penalized. If you step out of bounds, you lose the ball. If you trip another child on purpose, you are penalized because you have violated her rights. The coaches and the referees make the rules and all of the players agree to play by these rules before the game starts." (About this time your child may be wondering what you are getting at, so tell her. It is important during any disciplinary conversation to check that your child understands what you are trying to say.) "Erin, this is the way our home is going to operate. Everybody in our home has rights and we all need to respect each other's rights. Mom and Dad are going to make the rules, and as long as you are a member of the family you must abide by these rules. Just as in the soccer game, if you don't stick to the rules there are penalties." (You then describe what the rules are that come along with the corresponding penalties.) "As you get older the rules may change, just as the boundaries on your soccer field get longer and wider as you get older. But you must still stay inbounds."

Another important part of disciplining the older child is for both the mother and father to provide a united front in setting up the framework of discipline in the home. It is vitally important that the father sets the rules as to how the mother is to be treated. Here's an example of how I did this with our preadolescent son, Peter, who was in a rare defiant mood. He had been sassy to his mother during the day and when I heard about it that evening I took Peter aside and said to him, "Peter, I love your mother very much and I will not stand for you being disrespectful to her." (While I was talking to him, I was holding him firmly but lovingly on the shoulders and looking him squarely in the eye.) "Here is how I expect you to treat your mother ..."

In most homes mothers spend more time with the children than fathers, so it is important for the father to set the structure of the behavior that is expected in the home. There naturally will be a lot of overlap in many homes and the disciplinary roles are not so well defined anymore. It makes it much easier for the mother to carry out the discipline if the father has first set the limits and the children understand what these limits are.

Discipline based on love. Especially with older children it is important to drive home the point that you are

116

disciplining the child because you love him. Here is an example of how I convey this message of discipline and love with one of our older children, Peter.

"Peter, I love you very much. You never will realize how much a father loves his children until you have children of your own. Because I love you, there are certain goals I want you to achieve and one of these goals is that you obey Mom and Dad. This will help you someday reach your goal of being in charge of yourself, knowing what is right and wrong, and making the right decisions. The way I discipline you is very much like the way the spaceship, Apollo, reached the moon. The main reason that Apollo was able to reach the moon is that there were a lot of people at the space center in Houston constantly monitoring the path of that spaceship. If the spaceship strayed off the path, there was someone there, like a father, to guide the spaceship back on course. If there hadn't been anyone to guide the ship, it still would be going around in circles. Dad is going to be like one of those spaceship monitors. If I see you straying off course, I'm going to step in and help you get back on course. If I don't intervene, you're not going to reach your goals, you're not going to be very happy as a child, and I wouldn't be a very good father. Because I care about you very much, I'm going to stick by you to help you reach your goals. When you can set your own course, you won't need Dad to monitor you anymore. Even then it will be nice to know that you have a backup system on the ground in case your own controls fail."

Peter got the point that I was disciplining him because I love him.

32

THE FATHER'S ROLE IN
DISCIPLINE—TO SPANK
OR NOT TO SPANK

T o spank or not to spank is one of the most controversial
questions in discipline. I believe in correctly disciplining
a child; except in unusual circumstances, I do not believe
that spanking is wise. This opinion concerning discipline and
spanking is based upon experiencing 20 years in pediatric
practice and interacting with approximately 10,000 families,
rearing my own children, and discussing the spanking question with authorities knowledgeable in the field of child development. From this background, I have concluded that
spanking is at the bottom of the list of effective discipline
methods. Why? For two simple reasons: It seldom works and
it creates a distance between the father and child.

When I began writing parenting books a decade ago, I
honestly did not know whether spanking was right or not.
We seldom had cause in our own family to spank our children
and intuitively I always have felt that spanking was wrong.
Rather than simply give an opinion, however, I decided to
study the effects of spanking over the next ten years and have
made the following observations. Behavior that has been con-
trolled by spanking often results in angry children who operate from a basis of distrust rather than trust. Spanking leads
to a distance between the father and child. Children who
regard their father primarily as a "spanking disciplinarian"

tend to retreat from the father, to fear the father, and ultimately not to respect him as a loving authority figure.

Another reason for my lack of enthusiasm about spanking as a method of discipline is that it seldom works. In the hundreds of patients I have interviewed about spanking, most of them will, when pressed, admit that spanking does not work. This often results in spanking more and spanking harder and creating a greater distance between the parent and child.

Another argument against spanking is that this method of discipline often deprives a father from developing more creative and lasting methods of discipline. If you resort immediately to spanking, this is often the lazy way out. It keeps you from really getting to the reason your child exhibited undesirable behavior, developing methods for preventing this behavior from recurring, and leaving a lasting mental impression on your child rather than a physical impression.

The three goals of any disciplinary action are: (1) to stop an undesirable behavior; (2) to promote desirable behavior; and (3) to leave the child feeling right with himself and with the disciplinarian. Spanking may possibly accomplish the first goal, but that is all.

Spanking will not leave the child feeling right, especially when it is carried out in anger without regard for the child's feelings. It also does not focus on redirecting the child's future behavior. Spanking often is done to get the child to obey quickly, forgetting that true and lasting obedience is a long and gradual process beginning with the principles of nurturing and trust that I have discussed throughout this book. *Spanking may be a precursor to child abuse.*

There are some fathers who run a high risk for child abuse and definitely should use alternative methods of discipline other than spanking. These high-risk factors are: you were abused as a child, you have a high-need child (see Key 17), you are prone to impulsive anger, you find that spanking is not working, and you are spanking more often and harder. If you have any of these risk factors that might result in inappropriate spanking, I suggest you examine your entire father-child relationship.

However, it is unwise to give an absolute dictum that parents never should spank. This is not my purpose. There may be an occasional parent who has laid such a strong foundation of nurturing and trust with their child that spanking in certain circumstances does not harm the parent-child relationship. An example of such circumstance may be the child who willfully defies reasonable authority, although the rules have been given against the consequences of this action. Even parents who occasionally spank their children for reasons that they feel are justified find that this method of discipline is more effective only if based upon an early foundation of nurturing and trust. In my experience, spanking a child in whom you have *not* first laid this foundation of nurturing and trust does not work.

I have programmed myself against spanking. It is not in my discipline repertoire. However, I am committed to being a strong disciplinarian within our home. I will not let any wrong behavior go undisciplined. Because I am programmed against spanking I will exert more effort to develop ways of encouraging desirable behavior and more creative ways of disciplining undesirable behavior.

Some proponents of spanking argue that ancient writings support the use of the rod in disciplining children. I have studied thoroughly the root meaning of many of the rod verses in these ancient writings and have concluded that the "rod" could be interpreted as a tool for *guiding* the child, not beating the child.

33

~~~~~~

FATHERING THE ONE-TO THREE-YEAR-OLD

During this stage of development, the father's role widens from being a sensitive nurturer (during the first year) to a playful companion (from one to three years). Fathers really like this stage of development because their toddler finally can do something. During this stage, the child develops two important skills that make him more fun to be with: walking and talking. Fathering the one- to three-year-old is more enjoyable if dads first understand how children normally develop and what they do at this stage.

One of the most exciting developmental skills your child will develop at this age is the ability to talk. By speech I mean not only the verbal words but the entire art of body language, enabling a child to communicate his needs or wants and through this, stimulate adult responses. Just as it is important during the first year of development, the term *responsiveness* also is important during this stage of development. When a child gives verbal and body language cues, such as exclaiming, "Pick me up," while raising his hands, the more appropriately the parent responds, the more likely the child is to repeat this gesture. The response the child gets from his cues further stimulates him to refine his language because of the pleasant response it generates. As a result, he learns to talk better. By using his language to get an adult response, the child develops confidence and self-esteem.

If the child is not talking very much between one and two years of age, however, fathers may be frustrated. Although there is a wide variability in language development, most babies between one and two years old say little, but understand a lot. There are two aspects of language development: expressive—what a baby says, and receptive—what a baby understands. Receptive language precedes expressive language so your baby is understanding much more than you think he does. Some babies can say only a few words by fifteen months, but can understand simple directions such as, "throw the ball." By two years of age, most babies will understand much of what you say and will have a vocabulary of about 50 words, although these words sometimes are intelligible only to parents. Between two and three years of age, expect your child to show great strides in speech development, and to understand most of the simple play activities that you do with him.

Language Games To Enrich Your Child's Language Development:

Gesture games. Between two and three years of age, babies connect names and objects, such as ball, block, and baby. Once they make this connection, they respond to simple requests, such as, "Close the door," and "Pick up the ball." "No-no," however, usually is understood by a one-year-old. Your child learns by imitation. He hears sounds and attempts to parrot them. If the sound is accompanied by action, gestures, or objects, next he learns that these actions and objects have names. The formation of certain sounds, such as "Th" and "L," result in a variety of mouth contortions, tongue clicks, and jargon of various degrees of intelligibility. This jargon should neither be imitated nor corrected, but allowed to evolve. The child learns to correct sounds by repeatedly hearing the correct sound from his parents.

Fathers, because they often are less patient and sensitive to their child's early language struggles, often try to "correct" the toddler's speech too early. In correcting the toddler's speech, remember the main goal of toddler language is to communicate an idea, not a word. It is important for some babies to babble awhile and experiment with their own sounds without outside attempts to refine them. Toddlers simply are storing language information for a sudden rush of intelligible words and phrases that occurs at about two years. Much of a toddler's speech may be unintelligible under the age of two. This is normal. If you sense your child is having trouble with certain words, make a special effort to repeat these sounds frequently yourself and *capitalize on your child's desire to imitate.*

Let your child imitate correct speech. Infants learn speech by imitating the speech of their care givers. Don't use too much "baby talk." Talk with your infant in the language you want him to learn. Fathers seem to use more adult language with their baby, as if they have high expectations. This balance of different ways of talking to babies is good for the child's language development. Word games and action songs make language fun. Babies love to play games about their own body parts and quickly will learn what their toes are after they have played "This Little Piggy" several times. Rhythm games that employ counting and finger play, such as, "One, Two, Buckle My Shoe," will hold the toddler's interest. Action songs, such as "Pop, Goes the Weasel," particularly are helpful for encouraging gestures and cue words. For example, if you repeat "Pop, Goes the Weasel" several times and jump up and down, when your child hears the word "Pop," he will jump up by himself.

Correct by repetition, not by embarrassment. Once your child masters the art of sounds heard, objects seen, and sound imitation, his language has a snowball effect. After the toddler has a basic repertoire of about a dozen words, he keenly practices these words by repetition according to how much he is encouraged. Your toddler's initial speech repertoire may be simple nouns like "car." He then picks up on gestures associated with these sounds and adds action words, such as "go bye-bye" to his vocabulary. His next advance is to connect these isolated words to create meaningful phrases so his efforts resemble a budget telegram, for example, "bye-bye car." He associates "bye-bye" with leaving the house (which he learns from your gestures when you depart) and "car" as the moving object that transports him from one world to another.

Read to your child. At about one year of age, begin looking at picture books together. After pointing to the picture and repeating the name of the object, your child will develop his word-object association. Point to objects in the book and relate them to the real world, such as pointing to the tree in the book and the tree in the real world. As your child advances, select increasingly stimulating books that are appropriate to the next stage of speech development. Stimulate his recall of the names in the book by pointing to an object and saying, "What's this?" Show him an entire page of assorted objects and ask, "Where is the ball?"

Expansion is a key to enriching your child's language. Expand a word into an idea. For example, if a child asks, "What's that?" and points to a bird, you answer, "That's a bird." And you add, "Birds fly in the sky." You not only have answered his question and he has gained a word for the object, but you have also given him a word-associated idea that birds fly in the sky.

Give choices. Give your child frequent choices. For example, "Do you want an apple or an orange?" This not only obliges him to reply, but also stimulates the thought process of decision making.

Keep your speech simple. Speak slowly in simple sentences and pause frequently to give your child time to reflect on the message.

Eye-to-eye contact is very important during speech. If you maintain eye contact with your child, you can maintain his attention. Eyes have a unique language all their own, and you want your child to be comfortable speaking into another person's eyes. The ability to be comfortable with eye-to-eye contact is a language enrichment exercise that will benefit your child the rest of his life.

Locomotion—walking, running, and climbing. Besides language development, the next important skill that appears during this age is locomotion—walking, running, and climbing. This skill opens up whole avenues of fun activities between the father and child and also opens up another role of the father—designer of the child's environment. Playing architect is fun with your two- to three-year-old. Children at this age enjoy stacking, scribbling, building, and working with clay. Children between two and three years of age love to build things with Dad.

One of our most memorable Christmases took place when I was still in pediatric training. We could not afford expensive toys for our children, who were then two and four years old. I went down to a local lumberyard and for $2 I was able to fill the whole back of a station wagon with scraps of 2 by 4s, 4 by 4s, and other assorted short pieces of wood. I brought them home, sanded them a bit, stacked them in interesting ways, and called them building blocks. Our children enjoyed playing with these blocks longer than most of the plastic gadgets they received on subsequent Christmases.

34

~~~~~~

FATHERING THE THREE- TO SIX-YEAR-OLD

B y the time your child is three years of age, you and she together have built what I call "the fundamental person." By this, I mean that your child has graduated from each stage of development and is a better person for the skills she has acquired, the problems she has solved, the emotions she has felt and expressed, and the attachments she has made. By age three she is aware of her total self—what she feels, what she can do, what she is comfortable doing, what she cannot do. By age three, she has defined her role in the family and has mastered using her parents as support resources. Most children at this age have acquired the necessary motor, language, adaptive, and social skills. They are fun to be with!

The child who enters this stage of development will refine the basic skills learned in the first three years. A child who is deficient in any or all of these basic skills by age three must expend energy learning or relearning these skills, and is always playing catch up. This is why throughout this book I have emphasized the importance of *father involvement* during the early years of a child's life. The years between ages three and six usually are smoother on both parents and child. The refinement of acquired skills usually produces less anxiety than the struggles necessary for their acquisition during the first few years.

The impulsive and tantrum-like behavior of the two- to three-year-old gradually diminishes and you will notice your child's behavior becoming less impulsive. Your three-year-old has a language repertoire to effectively communicate her desires and feelings. She understands you and feels you understand her. This language facility results in less tantrum-like behavior because she is able to express her negative feelings with words rather than actions. Her behavior becomes less impulsive and more directed. It seems that her abilities finally have caught up with her desires. Mastering language adds the finishing touch to the attachment feelings your child has for you and begins the *social rapport stage* between parent and child. Your child simply is fun to talk with, take walks with, and play word-games with. At this stage, your child may assume the role of a close friend, a pal who is fun to be around. Children of ages three and four thrive on new experiences that seem arranged just for them. When our son, Matthew, was four years old he called this, "something special"—a desired or surprise activity for which he was singled out. This "something special" gains importance as the number of children in your family increases.

Dad as a social director. At this stage, your role widens to include molding your child's social environment. From three years on, a child begins to associate with others outside the family circle. Keep the finger on the pulse of your child's social relationships and, as much as possible, direct him into relationships with children whose behavior exemplifies your family values. This is especially true when it comes to aggressive behavior. Children at this impressionable age should not learn to fight their way through life, to be tough or "street smart." Teaching a child to be too tough, too young usually results in an unhealthy balance of aggression and not enough tenderness.

I feel that a child's values and behaviors should be established firmly in the first six years. On this basis, he will begin to question those values and experiment with some of his own. A child should not be exposed to violence and aggression (especially on television) at an age when he is not able to make value judgments about these behaviors. In the next stage of development, between six and twelve years, a child usually can begin to make these judgments. However, some fathers may feel they want their child to learn about "real life" at an early age, thinking that this prepares him better for the real world. We do not and never will live in an ideal society, but I do feel that the young child should grow up knowing what the ideal is or should be. At a later age he will realize and be able to cope with the fact that not all ideals can be attained.

Give your child the right values. The beauty of three- to six-year-olds is they are totally receptive to their parents' values. They seldom question what is right and wrong and willingly accept authority. It is vitally important to plant values at this age because in subsequent stages, as children go to school and become more independent of you, they begin to question your values, add those of peer relationships, and form some of their own. Children who do not have a solid foundation of home values by age six are left to flounder in a sea of uncertain values and are prone to accept those of peers, television influences, and a whole parade of outside value makers.

This stage is also a good time for a child to have a lot of one-on-one social contacts with Dad. Here is a tip for busy fathers: Take your child out to breakfast one day a week before work. With my daughters, I call this a "daddy-daughter date." Children at this age realize that dads are busy, so taking time out to do something with them really hits home. No matter how many discipline problems you may be having with your child, make these special times strictly for fun and communication. Save the criticism and chastening of undesirable behavior for another time.

Children like to help Daddy during this stage, washing the car, planting the garden, cutting grass. Doing helpful tasks with Dad is fun; doing them alone is work. There will come a time when you need to delegate chores to a child. If you get your child accustomed to working with you at an early age, it will be easier to assign the work to her when she is older.

Gender identity. Gender identity becomes apparent during this stage and distinct behavioral differences between the sexes appear. Generally speaking, boys are more aggressive and engage in more active play than girls of the same age. I feel that both genetic and cultural influences play an important role in this early gender identity.

Motor development. Fathers often are very interested in the motor development of children at each stage. The three-year-old usually has developed lateral and directional concepts. He throws and catches, runs, turns, and pivots with confidence. His walking assumes an adult-like gait. Climbing is still a favorite sport and jumping off greater heights is a typical three-year-old challenge. He becomes aware of how much physical abuse his developing bones and muscles can constantly handle and begins to learn to protect himself from injury. The development of his motor ability allows him to become more domesticated. He feeds himself with greater care, brushes his teeth, washes and dries his hands, cleans up after himself, dresses himself, and begins learning the task of managing the buttons on his apparel.

35

~~~~~~

FATHERING THE SIX-
TO ELEVEN-YEAR-OLD

T he child from six to eleven years of age enjoys a certain personality equilibrium. By this stage, he is secure in his position within the family, he has developed some social attitudes, and he has acquired some preliminary educational skills at home or in preschool. Middle childhood marks the beginning of a child's more formal education and refinement of his social attitudes. Although the family remains the center of his world, he reaches out for social relationships and peer acceptance and may spend the greater part of his day in pursuits outside the home. In order to enrich his self-esteem and emerging personality, your child has two special needs at this age—the need for social relationships and peer acceptance and the need for school success.

Peer dependence. At this stage, children's behavior and values are affected greatly by their peers. Because your child does not yet have the wisdom to tune out the values that are contrary to what you have taught him, it is necessary for fathers to keep tabs on what children are learning from others. The more your child is involved with other children, the more you need to get involved with your child. The enforcement of family values is especially important during middle child-hood so that your child enters adolescence firmly grounded in these values. A child who enters adolescence without strong values is confused easily and is more likely to adopt an undesirable value system.

Here are some ways you can become wisely involved in your child's social life during this stage:

Success. Your child needs success at this age. Create an environment in which your child's strong points are allowed to flourish. Is he good at a certain sport or a certain musical instrument? Identify these talents and encourage them. Every child needs to be good at something.

Get to know your child's interests and capabilities. Encourage his interests. You may wish your child to have certain interests that you feel are healthy for him. He must be allowed to pursue his own particular interests (providing, of course, they involve basically desirable behavior).

Welcome friends into your home. Your child's home is his castle too! This is the place where he is most secure and confident and where he can use his security to his social advantage, especially if he is a shy or withdrawn child. Your child is more likely to be a successful player if the game is played in his park. If your child succeeds at home, he is more likely to succeed away from home. Encourage your child to invite a friend to spend the night at home, thereby encouraging one-on-one social interaction in a secure environment.

Father as sports coach. A wonderful way to get to know your child (and what children are generally like at any given age) is to coach a sport. Being a coach gave me a lot of insight into my son. I learned about his abilities, his weaknesses, how he performed under pressure, and how his skills improved from the beginning of the season to the end. He also learned the same about me: my weaknesses, abilities, and control (or lack of it) under pressure. Getting involved in a sport with your child allows a father and child to learn about each other in a social setting. Many dads may not have the time or ability to coach their child's team, but you can get involved in other ways. You don't have to be an expert in a sport simply to show up and watch. Let your child know that what he is doing is important to you because he is important to you. Sports can bring out the best and worst in a child and in a father.

The sport should fit the child. A sport well suited to a child can bring out the best in him. A poor fit can bring out the worst. Some children have athletic bodies, some children are more physical, some are more cerebral, and some excel in both kinds of activities. Every child can and should excel in something. Periodically take inventory of how your child is doing on the team. Encourage your child to become involved in a sport that he or she wants, according to his or her own preferences and abilities. This choice may be different from yours. If the child doesn't fit the sport and continues not to fit, help her choose other activities in which she will be successful. Be cautious in making hasty decisions about pulling a child out of a sport. Children show a wide range of maturity at any given age. I have seen a "klutz" at the beginning of the season become well coordinated by the end.

Keep your finger on the pulse of your child's participation and wait for her skills to mature. Sports have a carryover effect in helping the child to succeed in other areas. Some children who are doing poorly academically may have their self-esteem boosted by their success in sports. *Dads, sports are for girls, too!* Gone are the days when organized sports were for boys only and girls were left to be passive observers.

One of the healthiest changes in the sports programs is the equal opportunity now offered to girls. Participation in organized sports helps to better prepare a child—son or daughter—for the future job market. Many of the leadership qualities necessary in business management are similar to those used in team leadership. I once heard a management executive complain that one of the difficulties women have in upper management is with team leadership, a quality that they could have developed better if they had participated more in organized team sports. Fathers need to keep an eye on their daughter's sports activities even more than their son's. There is a difference between being assertive (demanding your rights without infringing upon someone else's) and being aggressive (infringing upon someone else's rights). Competitive sports should teach girls to be assertive, but not aggressive, in their relationship with others.

If you participate in your child's sport, expect to be a taxi service. One of the problems of the modern father is not having enough time with his child. Taxiing your child and his teammates to and from games gives you extra time with your child. You can learn a lot about your child's level of self-esteem by noticing how he behaves in a car full of his contemporaries. This valuable time together is not wasted. Take advantage of it.

Your child needs your approval. It is common for a child during this middle childhood stage to withdraw periodically from family interests and, on the surface, not appear to care what you think of him or her. Don't undervalue how much your child craves your approval. Our son, Peter, recently brought this fact home to me. Peter was in a school play and I took my place in the audience as an admiring father. This happened to occur on the evening of a busy day and I was very tired. My thoughts during Peter's play were preoccupied with my patients. After the play, Peter seemed to withdraw from me. I finally found out what was bugging him when he confessed, "Dad, when I looked at you in the audience, you weren't watching me." Fathers have a way of being present physically, but absent mentally. Children also have a way of perceiving where your mind is.

133

Dad as business consultant. A child's desire to earn money emerges during middle childhood. Business ventures not only will teach your child about making money, they also teach responsibility, mathematics, economics, and a few social graces. For example, our eight-year-old daughter, Hayden, and our eleven-year-old son, Peter, decided to set up a small produce stand on a busy corner near our home. I agreed to act as their "business consultant," and they operated the stand. They first had to decide how much to charge for the tomatoes and zucchini they planned to sell so they went to the neighborhood supermarket to find out the going rate for these items. They painted a sign and, along with their box of produce and a scale, went into business. In order to make the situation more like a real store and to encourage them to use the math they had learned in school, I suggested that they sell the tomatoes by the pound rather than the easy way, so much per tomato. I realized how much Peter had absorbed about the real world of advertising and commerce when he bribed his four-year-old sister, Erin, to sit next to him adorned in a pretty pink dress, in order to lure more customers to the stand. How much fun it is to see children practicing what they learn from adults!

36

FATHERING THE TEENAGER

Adolescents are very active. They have enormous energy, often unbridled and undirected. "My son is like an eagle. The nest is too small and I can no longer hinder his flight," is how one father described his relationship with his teenager. Fathers can help channel this energy into meaningful activities that teenagers can handle. Adolescents sometimes overextend themselves with too many commitments and often they don't realize that they are in danger of burning out. A wise father can help the overextended teenager be more selective about his involvement in various activities.

Go with the flow. Teenagers vacillate between acting like children and acting like young adults. They are not completely comfortable with either role. Go along with your adolescent: When she wants to be a child, support her as you would a child; when she wants to be an adult, respect this desire too.

Be approachable. If your teenager gets a busy signal from you, she will quit calling. Even though much of her world lies beyond the walls of your home, your teenager must feel that the door is always open to her and that you can be approached for advice. Don't expect clear signals from your adolescent. She is unlikely to say, "Dad, I would like to have your undivided attention for the next ten minutes." Many times during the writing of this book one of our teenagers would stop at my desk and ask, "How's it going, Dad?" If I gave her a one word answer and kept on writing, the conversation would have ended right there. If, however, I looked her in the eye, shut down the word processor, turned, and put my feet on the desk, meaningful conversation often would follow. It was up to me to relay the message that I was willing to switch channels and give her some time.

Adolescents are impulsive. At a time when responsibility for the child's behavior is shifting from parental control to self-control, unchecked impulses often lead teenagers down undesirable paths and into unwise decisions. The teenager must begin to take full responsibility for the consequences of his decisions and must struggle to make those decisions wisely. Here's where early involvement with your child really pays off. If you have helped your child internalize your family value system by being an involved parent and by modeling the behavior you want him to follow, he will have the resources he needs to make wise decisions that will make you proud of him.

I explained this decision making process to our oldest son, Jim, something like this: "Jim, life is a series of decisions. One of the things that I wish for you is that you develop the wisdom to make the right decisions. I believe that within every person there is an inner guidance system, something like the governor on the speedometer of our car—the buzzer goes off when we go too fast. This system can help you check your impulses when you are tempted to act without thinking about the consequences. If you aren't sure which path to take, make a 'pretend' decision and then live with it for a few days. If your inner guidance system continues to tell you that it was the right decision, then go ahead and make that your final decision. But if the buzzer goes off and you have the gut feeling that your decision wasn't right, then change it. If you develop your inner guidance system and heed its warnings, you won't go wrong. If you don't listen to those inner feelings, you'll desensitize yourself to your own wisdom and you'll end up being indecisive or you'll make some very important wrong decisions."

Disciplining the teenager. During adolescence, the father's disciplinary role shifts gradually from administering corrective measures to being a counselor. You're there to listen and react and guide, not to force your child to obey you just because you are the father. It is important that your child perceives you as a wise counselor, even if there are times when you may not feel so wise. You are still an authority figure to your child, but the adolescent has learned that authorities are not infallible. *Listen carefully and explain your thoughts and feelings when you offer advice.* This will increase your chances that your teenager will listen to and follow your guidance. It's important that your child respects his mother's wisdom as well. It helps if dads point out that mothers are deeply intuitive about their children and that even if they don't completely understand that intuition, they grow to respect it. I've told our older sons always to be truthful and straightforward with their mother, because she can see right through them and won't hesitate to say so. It is healthy for children of all ages, especially adolescents, to feel that Dad truly respects Mom. To improve communication in our discipline, I have made a "deal" with our children: "No matter what you do, if you tell Dad about it I will not get angry." This promise not to get angry has helped them to be free to communicate feelings and actions with me that they may otherwise have not. They don't expect me always to approve of what they do, but I have promised not to get angry as long as they open up.

Car-key discipline. In some ways I find older teenagers easy to handle. I have something they want—the car keys.

The car keys have some strings attached to them. If my teenagers want the car keys from me, I have to see a certain kind of behavior from them. Some people call this bribery, but it works.

The privilege-responsibility ratio. Another part of disciplining a teenager is handing out privileges and responsibilities in the right ratio. Keeping a reign on your teenager means knowing when to let out and when to pull in. A teenager must appreciate the relationship between privileges and responsibility—with increasing privileges come increasing responsibilities. Only when the teenager shows he can handle the responsibilities does he get the increase in privileges. Teenagers are egocentric enough without their parents giving them a free ride when it comes to household and familial responsibilities. Being given responsibility is important in developing self-discipline and self-guidance.

Parents influence a teenager, but should not control. When you're the father of teenagers, you have to face the fact that you cannot completely control their behavior. Most of their time is spent with people and institutions outside of the home: school, peers, church, television, entertainers, and so on. You have to make an effort to keep in touch. Here is a suggestion: At least once a month, take your teen out for some one-on-one time and really make an effort to talk about what's going on in his or her life. When you pry a bit, don't worry that your teenager will think that you are being nosy. What he does is important to you because he *is* important to you. Most teenagers become increasingly quiet about their lives. However, in my years of counseling teenagers, I have heard more complaints about parents who are too little involved rather than too much.

During these outings, provide a setting that allows your teenager to ventilate his feelings. One of the most common complaints teenagers share with me is, "My dad doesn't understand me. He doesn't even try." Another is, "My dad doesn't understand my position." To help overcome these feelings try to first *listen to your child's position,* offer some understanding comments, and if you do not approve, tell him why. At least you have given him the message that you are willing to hear his positions and "deal" a bit.

These special times with your teenager are like taking inventory in your business. Just as in business, it's important to know where you stand with your child and where your child stands with herself. But don't go too far. A concerned mother once confided in me, "My husband tries to run our child like he runs his corporation. He tries to manipulate her and control her and seldom tries to understand her point of view." Children are not corporations. *They have private lives that should be respected.*

Fathers can help build an adolescent's self-esteem. A teenager's self-esteem is based upon how he perceives others perceiving him. Although peer acceptance is high on the teenager's list, you can help his self-image by making him feel truly esteemed at home. Make sure your teenager does not feel his value is tied to his accomplishments.

QUESTIONS AND ANSWERS

Our two-and-a-half-year-old son plays with dolls. This bothers me. I want our boys to grow up to be real boys and our girls to be real girls. Am I right?

Defining masculinity and femininity is difficult without succumbing to cultural stereotyping. We are led to believe that the term masculine means assertive, decisive, physical, deliberate, and logical. Femininity often is associated with sensitivity, warmth, expressiveness, and ego building qualities. Perhaps it is more accurate to state that one set of traits predominates in a healthy masculine or feminine identity, but that each sex possesses some or all of the qualities in both categories. It is fair to say that fathers are more concerned about masculine and feminine behaviors than mothers. A father may give a boy a football expecting him to kick it and give a daughter a doll expecting her to cuddle it. When the son cuddles the football and the daughter kicks the doll, the father's well-laid plans go astray. Mothers may give dolls or stuffed animals to cuddle or nurture to either boys or girls. You should realize that the fact that you and your wife approach the teaching of sex roles differently can result in a healthy balance for your child. Fathers seem to steer the child to more predominantly one sex role, whereas mothers allow the child to adopt some qualities associated with both sexes. Like so many aspects of parenting, the key issue here is *bal-*

ance. Let your boy play with dolls as well as other toys. Boys need to develop tenderness too.

I am a new father with money worries. I am the only breadwinner in the family and my wife wants to be a full-time mother, but I worry about making ends meet. Any suggestions?

Your concerns about being the breadwinner are a normal part of the profession of fathering, and apparently you take this profession seriously. You have chosen the traditional family economic structure with the father as the only breadwinner—a decision that is becoming more and more difficult for many families in today's world. Here are some suggestions to help you juggle family finances, your job, and time with your family.

Verbalize your worries to your wife so that she can understand and help you make some basic financial decisions. It helps when both husband and wife are in agreement about where to cut financial corners. Basically you both are making the decision that family relationships are much more important than material things. Decide together which things you temporarily can do without, what you must have, how much you can afford. Take the leadership in the family by conveying to your wife that you feel it is more important that you have time with your family than to take a second job or work longer hours to earn extra income. This is a trade-off that you are asking your wife to accept. Although you may have less money, you are asking your wife to value your role as an active participant in child care, not only as a breadwinner. In my experience, most mothers place a higher value on having an involved father than in bringing home a fatter paycheck.

141

Part of your growth and development as a new father is to learn to balance your financial commitment to your family with the commitment to your child. If there is no way you can make ends meet when you are the only breadwinner, then consider having your wife supplement the income by finding a way to work at home. The possibilities are endless; a few ideas to get you thinking are: child care, telephone soliciting, typing, word processing, catering, tutoring, and home businesses, such as mail order or sewing. (A good reference text that discusses many alternatives to working outside the home and earning extra income at home is the book *The Heart Has Its Own Reasons*, published by La Leche League International, Franklin Park, Illinois, 1986.)

My job requires me to travel a great deal. I don't like it, but I am committed to finishing a project that requires me to be away one or two days a week for the next few months. We have a one-year-old and we are very close. What can I do to maintain this attachment even though I have to travel?

Your dilemma is shared by thousands of traveling fathers who miss being with their babies, yet realize their importance as the breadwinner. As one traveling father of a large family put it, "Someone has to fund this operation!" Try leaving as much of yourself behind as possible and use all the latest technology to maintain contact with your wife and baby while you are away. Leave tape recordings of yourself singing a bedtime song to your baby and a "father loves you" message. Be sure to use phrases in songs that your baby associates with you. Leave photographs of yourself.

Mothers have told me that often they bring out the pictures and tape recordings (audio and video) of Dad during those moments of the day when the baby seems particularly fussy. Bringing back memories of Dad seems to soothe the baby during a fussy period, as if she reflects upon the memory of a special person who is missing. Call and talk to your child frequently, especially before bedtime. When she gets older, you may even call this the "surprise call." Telling a bedtime story by phone is a winner. In fact, it is quite common for mothers to get a bit fussy when Dad is away because one of their major support people is not around.

Do not be disappointed if your baby gives you a temporary cold shoulder when you return. Babies feel a mixture of anger and confusion about Dad being away, and may need some time to adjust to your return. To smooth your reentry, don't immediately come on too strong, but gradually re-bond with your baby by clicking her into one of her favorite fun activities with you. Hold her in one of her favorite ways and sing one of her favorite songs. Soon you will strike a familiar note and have a happy reunion.

I want to be involved in the birth of our baby and help make my wife's labor as comfortable as possible. How can I help her?

Your role in childbirth is to ensure, as much as you are able, that your wife has the opportunity to follow the natural signals of her body during childbirth. Attending natural childbirth classes helps her tune into her body signals and helps you understand and be prepared for the various stages of labor and delivery. Often the schedules and routines of hospital labor and delivery units do not encourage mothers to truly follow their body signals, so this is where you can play an important role.

Encourage your wife to move around during labor. Help her assume the laboring position in which she feels the most comfortable. Help her try standing, sitting, walking the halls, leaning over a table, getting on all fours, even squatting. Lying on her back during most of her labor is not only the most uncomfortable position for a mother, but may also slow the progress of labor. Be tuned in to your wife's needs. Be ready with pillows when she needs them for support. Rub her back. (A 4-inch paint roller is excellent for back massage.) Spare your wife the hassles. A laboring woman is not always rational and diplomatic with the attending medical personnel. She shouldn't have to be. Her focus should be on her own needs and her body's signs. Any hassles with the attending personnel (hospital policies, routines, paperwork) should be taken care of by you. Remember, too, a laboring mother is particularly vulnerable to suggestions that she may not be making progress as fast as expected. ("Tsk, tsk, still only two centimeters dilated.") If you sense a negative dialogue developing between your wife and the attending personnel, step in and redirect the communication in a more positive direction. In essence, do what a father does best, love and care for your wife.

I've heard a lot about mothers getting depressed after birth, but I'm starting to feel a bit depressed myself. Can fathers experience postpartum depression?

Yes, but in a different way. Although fathers do not experience the physical and hormonal changes that mothers do, they have unique adjustment problems too. Your postpartum adjustment problems are probably due to your suddenly increased responsibilities and dramatic changes in lifestyle. You have another mouth to feed, your wife is never going to act the same or be the same, and you probably will never have as much time with your baby and wife as you want to have. Many fathers are overwhelmed by having to take care of a new baby and be a husband to their wife—who needs a bit of mothering herself. The demands of fathering a baby and mothering a mother may be too much too soon and result in depression. It is an awesome responsibility to hold a major part of the outcome of another human being in your hands. It helps to focus more on the joys of fathering rather than just the responsibilities. Realize the fun you are now having and will continue to have with your baby. This fun will change with every change of your baby's development, and your development. If you allow it to flow naturally, your baby will give to you as much as you give to him. Also, don't let yourself be so preoccupied with the things you must get for your baby that you lose sight of your interactions with him that will profit him more than the toys you buy. Give of yourself. It's much better and less expensive.

I love to touch and massage our baby's skin. I notice that he responds differently to my touch than to my wife's. Is this my imagination or can six-month-old babies really feel the difference?

Yes, they can—and it's a good difference to feel. Mothers and fathers intuitively touch and massage their babies differently. Mothers tend to use more of their fingertips and a lighter stroke, whereas fathers tend to use their whole hand. Try the following massage tips.

Place your baby, unclothed, on a soft surface, such as a lambskin. Be sure the room is warm and your hands are warm (immerse your hands in warm water and dry them before starting, or rub them together vigorously to increase the heat to your palms). Warm the baby oil by placing a small amount in your hands and vigorously rubbing your hands together. Babies like wide, circular strokes. Start with the neck and then gradually do the limbs, stroking from the shoulder all the way to the tips of the fingers and from the groin to the soles of the feet. Tense babies have tense limbs. When you see your baby's fists gradually unfolding and his limbs dangling limply from his sides, you know your soothing massage is getting through to him.

I will soon become a grandfather for the first time. My daughter wants to stay home, but has to go back to work after a few months because her husband is still a student and they need the money. I want to help, but I don't want to interfere. Is it right to give them some money?

Yes. Let me share with you a recent story about one of my patients. Jack, a stockbroker friend, frequently would call with the advice, "Doc, I've got a good investment for you." Shortly after Jack became a grandfather for the first time and his daughter was in a similar working dilemma as yours, I called him and said, "Jack, I've got the best investment tip you've ever heard." I went on to advise him that the best investment in his grandchild's future would be to give or loan the new couple enough money to allow his grandchild to have the best start in life—the interaction with a full-time mother. He thanked me and made the investment.

There is a historical precedent for this type of investment. In many cultures it used to be and sometimes still is customary to give an inheritance to couples when they become new parents rather than after the death of a grandparent. Financial pressures are one of the greatest stresses on today's young parents. Grandparents can help a lot. Besides financial assistance, grandparents can offer to baby-sit. Mothers returning to work feel much better about their situation when they trust their substitute care giver.

Our baby is one month old and my wife seems to be going downhill. She isn't taking care of herself and is getting

downright sloppy about her grooming. What can I do to help?

Many women suffer a body image problem after birth. They don't feel as attractive, and they don't feel they have the time for good grooming. This is part of the "my-baby-needs-all-of-me" syndrome. This syndrome is not only a normal by-product of most committed mothers, but may also be a sign of early burnout. You may need to step in and insist that she take time out to take care of herself. Here are some specific tips on how to help your wife take better care of herself so that ultimately she can take better care of baby.

Make an appointment for her to have a facial or something she enjoys and drive her there. Be sure you market this as something for her good, and not yours, or she may fall victim of the common feeling of "I'm not as attractive to you as I used to be, so you want to fix me up." It really helps if you try to share in the overall care of your baby as much as possible. The more you prove yourself capable of sensitively caring for your baby, the more your wife will let go of her baby and take better care of herself. In my survey of the causes of mother burnout, I have found that one of the most precipitating causes is an uninvolved and insensitive husband.

I have not been an involved father and my child is now two years old. I now realized what I missed. Is it too late to become involved with his care and how do I make up for lost time?

It is never too late to begin building a relationship with your child. Throughout this book, I stress the importance of early involvement because the earlier you become involved the easier it is to get hooked on fathering. Many fathers, including myself, do not realize the importance of early involement and they leave most of the baby care to the mother. It took me four children to learn what I had missed. Because you have not taken a major role in the care of your baby early on, it is natural for you to feel a bit uncomfortable taking charge of your baby and it is normal for your baby to not easily warm up to you. With time, both of these interactions will improve. Simply get your hands on your baby more. Play with him, comfort him, take him places with you, console him when he wakes up at night, put him to bed, feed him, and bathe him. Interactions with your baby build a relationship. The more you interact with your baby the more comfortable you will become in baby care and the more easily your baby will warm up to you. Babies are very resilient. They give us a second chance at bonding with them.

I am a priority father; my family comes first. I enjoy spending nearly all of my free time with my family and don't go out with the guys much. How can I handle the flak I'm getting at work?

You don't have to apologize to anyone for your style of fathering. You wisely have committed yourself to the wisest investment you'll ever make—your family. Your friends may not understand how you can derive so much enjoyment from your family. Down deep they probably are envious that they did not make the same priority decisions that you have. Be proud of the choice you have made.

GLOSSARY

Attachment fathering the style of fathering in which a dad shares the care of the baby and continues his strong involvement with the child.

Doula a woman who assists the laboring mother during childbirth and/or cares for her needs after the baby is born.

Engrossment the absorption, preoccupation, and interest that a newborn evokes from a father.

Family council a disciplinary and family communication tool activated by calling together family members for an informal discussion.

Freeway fathering the art of lulling a baby to sleep in a car seat by the constant motion and sound of the car during a nonstop ride for at least 20 minutes.

Labor coach assisting the laboring woman to use her body to ease the pain and to speed the progress of labor.

Laying on of hands the bedtime ritual of the father placing his hands on "the bulge" of his wife's abdomen and talking to the pre-born baby.

Neck nestle the art of comforting the baby by nestling the baby's head into the father's neck, with the father's neck and chin draping over the baby's head.

Reciprocity synchronized movements between the parent and baby when the baby's body movements are in synchrony with inflections in the parent's voice, as if each is taking turns talking.

INDEX

DR. BALTER'S STEPPING STONE STORIES
Dr. Lawrence Balter,
Illustrations by Roz Schanzer

Each of the storybooks in this series deals with a particular concern a young child might have about growing up. Each book features the same cast of characters—the kids who live in the fictional town of Crescent Canyon, a group to whom any youngster can relate. The stories are thoroughly entertaining while they help kids to understand their own feelings and the feelings of others. Engaging full-color illustrations fill every page! (Ages 3–7) Each book: Hardcover, $5.95, 40 pp., 8" x 8"

A Funeral for Whiskers:
Understanding Death ISBN: 6153-5

A.J.'s Mom Gets a New Job:
Adjusting to a Separation ISBN: 6151-9

Alfred Goes to the Hospital: Understanding a Medical Emergency ISBN: 6150-0

Linda Saves the Day:
Understanding Fear ISBN: 6117-9

Sue Lee's New Neighborhood:
Adjusting to a New Home ISBN: 6116-0

Sue Lee Starts School:
Adjusting to School ISBN: 6152-7

The Wedding: Adjusting to a
Parent's Remarriage ISBN: 6118-7

What's the Matter With A.J.?:
Understanding Jealousy ISBN: 6119-5

ISBN PREFIX: 0-8120

Books may be purchased at your bookstore, or by mail from Barron's. Enclose check or money order for total amount plus sales tax where applicable and 10% for postage and handling (minimum charge $1.75, Canada $2.00). Prices are subject to change without notice.

Barron's Educational Series, Inc.
250 Wireless Boulevard
Hauppauge, NY 11788
Call toll-free: 1-800-645-3476
In NY: 1-800-257-5729

IN CANADA:
Georgetown Book Warehouse
34 Armstrong Avenue
Georgetown, Ontario L7G 4R9
Call toll-free: 1-800-247-7160

BARRON'S

JUST FOR PARENTS AND PARENTS-TO-BE!

Barron's **PARENTING KEYS** is an informative series of fingertip references written especially for parents and parents-to-be. Each authoritative text is filled with advice from doctors and childcare experts on how to raise a child in today's world of time constraints and working couples. The books get right to the important points without sacrificing any pertinent information. Each book: Paperback, $5.95, 160 pp., 5¼" x 8¼"

Keys to Choosing Child Care
Stevanne Auerbach, ISBN 4527-0

Keys to Preparing and Caring for Your Newborn
William Sears, M.D. ISBN: 4539-4

Keys to Calming the Fussy Baby
William Sears, M.D. ISBN: 4538-6

Keys to Becoming a Father
William Sears, M.D. ISBN: 4541-6

Keys to Breast Feeding
William Sears, M.D. and Martha Sears, R.N., ISBN: 4540-8

Books may be purchased at your bookstore, or by mail from Barron's. Enclose check or money order for total amount plus sales tax where applicable and 10% for postage and handling (minimum charge $1.75, Canada $2.00). Prices are subject to change without notice.

Barron's Educational Series, Inc.
250 Wireless Boulevard
Hauppauge, NY 11788
Call toll-free: 1-800-645-3476
In NY: 1-800-257-5729

IN CANADA:
Georgetown Book Warehouse
34 Armstrong Avenue
Georgetown, Ontario L7G 4R9
Call toll-free: 1-800-247-7160

ISBN PREFIX: 0-8120

BARRON'S